MEDIA
MATTERS

How to leverage the media to grow your business

SCOTT MILLER

FREILING
PUBLISHING

Published by Freiling Publishing,
a division of Freiling Agency, LLC.
P.O. Box 1264
Warrenton, VA 20188

www.FreilingPublishing.com

Paperback ISBN: 978-1-956267-34-1
eBook ISBN: 978-1-956267-35-8

Printed in the United States of America

CONTENTS

INTRODUCTION

I HAVE ALWAYS been fascinated with media. From my earliest memories as a young boy, I recall playing music on a record player and pretending I was a radio station DJ. My music collection wasn't that great, but I loved the idea of radio.

Growing up in the Waco, Texas area, my dad was a grocery store manager. He would advertise his business on the local radio stations. Hearing my dad on the radio was so cool. The local station referred to my dad as "one-take Miller," in reference to the fact that he would record his commercial spot in one take. And when the radio stations did live remotes at Dad's store, you can bet I was the kid bothering the DJ.

One summer, Dad brought home a roll of butcher paper so I could use it for arts and crafts. I turned it into my first newspaper, complete with a sports section and comics. I had one subscriber—thanks, Mom.

When my family got our first VCR in the 1980s, I would pretend I was running a movie channel for cable and program the Saturday afternoon movie block. When I wasn't running the movie network, I would imagine my life as a TV show. This was before reality TV.

So, is it any surprise I chose media for a career? I have had the pleasure of working for local radio stations, streaming platforms, writing for newspapers, programming a national channel for SIRIUS Satellite Radio, running four national TV networks, hosting a national radio show and podcast, hosting a TV show, and writing a weekly blog.

When I was not pretending to be a media mogul, my other dream was opening a retail store that sold everything. I was going to call it "Stuff." Real original, I know. As a preteen I had a vision to open a large lawn mowing business, but "Scott's Lawncare" was already taken.

It wasn't until later in life that I realized my entrepreneurial drive. I love to create things from nothing or build something small into something big. I am blessed today that I can use my passion for both media and business in my role as CEO of a content marketing agency. I get to wake up every day and help business owners with their media needs.

But what I have discovered over the years is that while most business leaders know they need to be marketing their companies, they just don't know where to begin. There are three stages of knowledge. The first stage is "I don't know what I don't know." The second stage is "I know what I don't know." The final stage is "I know what I know." My goal is to help business leaders realize what they don't know, so they can begin to see how content media can help them grow their business.

This book breaks down the history and trends of different forms of media, experts give you insight into the changes and future of media, and you will receive practical tips to help you get started with content marketing on your own. I hope you enjoy reading this book as much as I have enjoyed writing it.

Scott Miller
August 20, 2021

1

THE CHANGING LANDSCAPE OF MEDIA

Video is Changing

I N THE SUMMER of 2021, a major news story broke in the world of college sports. The University of Texas and the University of Oklahoma were rumored to be leaving the Big 12 Conference for the SEC.

On the surface, this decision made no sense. UT Austin is one of the richest schools in the nation and OU had won the Big 12 Conference title in football for six consecutive years. The college football playoffs were talking about expanding the number of teams they invite every year, guaranteeing the Big 12 Champion a spot in the playoffs. With only ten schools in the Big 12, the split in annual revenue put UT and OU on par with other major college football brands. Was it a money decision? Perhaps. No doubt adding UT and OU to the SEC would garner more revenue. And you could argue the move was related to an NCAA decision to allow student athletes to monetize off of their name, image, and likeness. But I believe the move was more related to the changing landscape of media.

To understand how media is evolving, you must look first at the history. Before paid TV, the only way to watch sports was on one of three major broadcast stations. If ABC, CBS, or NBC were not airing the game, you had to listen to the game on the radio or read about it the next day in the newspaper.

According to the National Cable Television Association, the first cable system was introduced in 1948, but only delivered broadcast channels to Oregon, Arkansas, and Pennsylvania. In the 1970s and '80s the first TV networks debuted, including ESPN and the Regional Sports Networks. All of a sudden college sports were programming opportunities and the media companies started offering universities money for the rights to air their games.

My lead investor at Centerpost Media, Ed Frazier, founded one of our networks, BizTV, in August of 2009. But he is also one of the original leaders of the Regional Sports Networks. He told me about the time he made the decision to pay the Big 8 Conference forty million dollars for the rights to air their games. That meant the eight schools in the conference would split the forty million. To give you some perspective, each major university brings in at least forty million a year in rights today.

But how could ESPN and the Regional Sports Networks afford to pay universities huge checks for broadcasting rights? The answer is simple: cable networks acted like government agencies. In other words, they had a taxation model.

Think about how taxes work. You pay local, state, and federal taxes every year. Your tax dollars go to improving things like the roads you drive on to work. But you don't just pay for the roads you take; no, your tax dollars pay for all the roads.

That is how the cable TV system was created. You paid a monthly bill for a list of all the channels, not just the channels you watched. So if you were not a sports fan, but subscribed to cable to watch movies, you still paid for ESPN. To the tune of about seven dollars a month. A month! Do the math. According to a Los Angeles Times article from 2014, DirecTV had about twenty million US subscribers that year who were all paying seven dollars a month. That is $140 million a month that went to ESPN just from DirecTV. Not a bad cash flow.

In ESPN's defense, it costs a lot of money to produce live sports. And remember, they are writing big checks every year to universities and the professional sporting leagues.

But the TV consumer's needs started to shift in the new century. More and more subscribers started to ask for à la carte options. They no longer wanted to pay for channels they were not watching. As the internet speeds grew faster at home, new options for watching content started to grow, and the taxation model that had funded channels like ESPN started to evaporate quickly.

Leichtman Research Group, Inc. released a study that showed TV providers lost 4.9 million net video subscribers in 2019, pre COVID-19 pandemic. Do a quick search on Google and you will find several stats showing that the decline in paid TV subscribers to cable or satellite has been increasing each year. But if you just take the 4.9 million number, that is a loss of $411.6 million annually for a network like ESPN.

The industry needed an answer, and it came in the form of memberships, a new taxation model. ESPN's parent company Disney went on a spending spree buying major studio libraries like Marvel, Star Wars, and 20th Century Fox. The leaders at Disney knew that to survive the new media landscape, they needed to aggregate enough content to get enough consumers to subscribe to their platform Disney+. It worked. According to the New York Times, in 2021 (at the time this is being written) there were reportedly 116 million worldwide subscribers to Disney+, paying eight dollars a month. That is a new revenue stream of more than $11 billion a year.

ESPN is following their lead, on the hunt to gain as many major brands as possible under their umbrella of ESPN+. So going back to my earlier question, why would the University of Texas and the University of Oklahoma leave the Big 12 and join the SEC? The answer is money, but it is money coming from a future deal with ESPN and their need for all the major college brands.

What does this have to do with business? Everything. If you want to grow your brand you need to market your business. The traditional avenues of advertising your business are changing. As a business owner you need to understand these changes. You need to know where the consumer is going so you can spend your marketing dollars wisely.

There is more video content available today than there ever has been in the history of humankind. Think about all the different platforms where you can watch content. In the Miller house we have subscribed to YouTube TV, Hulu+, Disney+, ESPN+, Netflix, Apple TV+, and checked out services like Pluto TV, Peacock TV, and several others. In addition, we get more than ninety channels for free over the air. I think I spend more time trying to decide what I want to watch than I do actually watching TV!

This abundance of options means viewership is divided, making it increasingly harder to reach prospective customers. If you want to market your local business to women, ages thirty-five to fifty-five, where do you find them? Some are watching Netflix, some Hulu, and some are watching broadcast TV.

To further complicate matters, most of the streaming platforms are subscriber-based and don't air commercials. So how do you reach these prospects? We will dive more into the world of the growth of video platforms, including a resurgence of broadcast TV, in Chapter Four. And we will explore how TV advertising still works in Chapter Five. Finally, we will look at the new streaming platforms in Chapter Six.

Audio is Changing

In 2005, I was hired to build a Christian Talk Channel for SIRIUS Satellite Radio. This was before the merger with XM. After working in local radio for eight years, I was excited by the opportunity to work in the new medium.

What is old is often new again. When radio was in its golden years in the 1920s, you had three major networks: NBC Red, NBC Blue (which was later rebranded as ABC), and CBS. National networks meant the entire country could tune into the same program from coast to coast.

To me, what really made radio special was the local stations. You could tune in and listen to the play-by-play of the local high school football team on Friday nights, or your favorite college team on Saturdays. You knew what was happening in your community with the morning news report and you always knew how to dress for that day's weather. That all started to change with the passing of the Telecommunications Act of 1996, the same year I got my first radio job, as luck would have it.

The new law allowed companies to own multiple radio stations in a single market, opening the door for major corporations to buy most of the local stations. Publicly traded companies answer to shareholders and the pressure is there to cut expenses and increase revenue. I remember touring a radio station group in the late 1990s and seeing studio after studio sitting empty. When I asked where all the DJs were, it was explained how the morning show hosts all recorded mid-day shifts for other markets. And the mid-day DJs you heard in this market were all morning show hosts in other markets.

That was just the beginning. Soon the rise of more syndicated content started taking over the local airwaves. More and more stations became automated, to the point that the FCC had to invent a new way to make sure emergency broadcasts would air when needed. In the old Emergency Broadcast System (EBS), a message was sent to the local DJ who was required by law to read it on air. But with several empty studios, no one was there to read the message. The new Emergency Alert System (EAS) was automated.

Local radio hasn't died; there are still hundreds of stations providing local content today. But just like with video, the needs of the consumer have changed. We live in an on-demand world. My kids don't listen to local radio. They play music on Pandora (owned by SIRIUS-XM), Spotify, or Amazon Music.

The world of internet radio and on-demand music is once again dividing the prospective customers for business owners looking to market their business. When my dad was a grocery store manager in Waco, he bought ads on the two top-rated radio stations. I remember one Thanksgiving week there was a mix up and both stations were scheduled for a live remote at my dad's store. The parking lot was packed with people buying food for Thanksgiving. But how does a grocery store or any other business advertise via radio today?

And we haven't even touched on the growing trend of podcasts. Younger generations are not listening to talk radio, they are subscribing to their favorite podcasts.

I believe radio is not going away but will have to reinvent to survive in the future. We will discuss in detail how audio is changing, and how you can still use audio to market your business, in Chapter Three.

Written Media is Changing

BACK IN 2010 a friend of mine was poking fun at me, asking how old I was when I told him I still got a newspaper delivered to my front door. It has now been a few years since we paid for a newspaper subscription.

Pew Research data shows the number of subscribers to local newspapers today is almost half of what it was a decade earlier.

This used to be another reliable source for marketing your business. You could take a full, half, or quarter page ad to let the local community know what services and products you had to offer. Today your prospects are reading their news online through a variety of sources. Your local newspaper is focusing more and more on digital and national sites like Yahoo News to deliver daily email reminders to visit their website.

There are other sources of written media that are growing, like blogs. You might be surprised to know that book sales are increasing, thanks in large part to sites like Amazon. We will dive into the written media in more detail in the next chapter.

The Growing Trend Toward Online

I REMEMBER LOGGING onto the Internet for the first time as a freshman at Howard Payne University in 1996. I had used computers throughout my grade school years, but when I walked into that computer lab and logged onto the Internet, I was hooked. I looked up to realize I had been sitting at the computer for three hours straight.

The Internet has changed our lives. Today we have smartphones and smart watches with information available at our fingertips in seconds. What a world we live in where I can tell my wife that we need to order some supplies for our pool and have it delivered to my front door the same day. I guess we really are living the life of the cartoon Jetsons! But when do we get our flying cars?

The World Wide Web has been the biggest disrupter to media and how businesses market their companies. When you look at how we watch video, listen to audio, and read material, you can track it all back to the Internet.

It is great as a consumer! I geek out on technology. I love my iPhone, Apple watch, Alexa devices and my streaming boxes. I get in my car and tell my phone to call someone or start listening to an audio book. At home I ask Alexa to announce that dinner is ready or to add bread to my shopping list. I pick up my Apple TV, Roku, or Amazon Fire remote (yes, I have one of each in my home) and tell the remote to pull up movies starring Tom Cruise. I have my home cameras and alarm system pulled up on one phone app, I can order dinner in another, or order a ride to the airport in multiple other apps. I am living the tech lover's dream. As a side note, my wife of more than twenty years tolerates my obsession with technology, while my two teenage girls just roll their eyes at me (though that likely has little to do with the technology).

From a marketing standpoint, technology is great if you know how to utilize it. But you must understand who owns the Internet. You thought the Internet was a free resource available to everyone? He who controls the search engines controls the searches. We are going to discuss digital marketing in Chapter Nine, and how to properly list your business in Chapter Ten.

Social Media Has a Place

I THINK SOMEWHERE on the interwebs I still have a MySpace account. I never deleted it, so I assume it still exists. But our world changed in 2007 when Facebook came on the scene. Thanks to Mark Zuckerberg and the nerds at Harvard University I am now connected with everyone I ever knew in high school, college, and former places of employment.

Seriously, I have a love-hate relationship with social media. It is fun to see my friends' pictures of their kids growing up. I enjoy some of the funny memes. I mainly follow sports-related topics on Twitter. You will not find this Gen X on Snapchat or whatever new form of social media the kids are on. I hate all the hate. Do we really need to know everyone's opinion about everything? But that is social media.

Every now and again Facebook will show me my posts from the early years. I am sure my eighty-six friends I had in 2007 were so happy to read that I was eating lunch.

Social media is a very powerful tool that you can use to market your business, but relatively speaking it is still a new form of media, when you consider print, radio, and TV have all been around for decades. Social media is still a baby, so be careful when someone tells you they have years of experience with social media. But there are some things you can learn and use to your advantage. There are more things you need to learn to avoid when marketing your business on social media. We will discuss the do's and don'ts for you to consider in Chapter Eight.

Content Marketing is The Future

WHAT IS CONTENT marketing? According to Oxford Languages, content marketing is "a type of marketing that involves the creation and sharing of online material, such as videos, blogs and social media posts, that does not explicitly promote a brand, but is intended to stimulate interest in its products or services." Thanks, Oxford.

Full disclosure: I run a content marketing agency, so you know I am big on content marketing. I like Oxford's definition, but I would add that content marketing also exists on traditional media platforms like print, radio, and television. In fact, content marketing has been around for decades.

If you want to boil down my thesis for this book, it's that businesses need to have a content marketing strategy in order get the word out about their products or services in today's media environment.

Think of content marketing as building a loyal following of current and potential customers for your business. This is different from creating a commercial and airing it on radio or TV. This is creating a radio or TV show and building an audience. Content marketing can also be writing a weekly blog on your website and pushing it out to your clients. It can be a podcast that you record weekly. It can be a book that you publish. Or content marketing can be a series of videos you push out on social media. The key is your company creating content that people want to consume, and using that content to then educate prospects on your products and services.

So why is content marketing so key to today's overall marketing plan? There is an old saying in the media business: "Content is king." Think back to my example of all the different ways the consumer can watch video today. You can watch TV via YouTube TV, Sling TV, DirecTV, Dish, Cable TV, Prime TV, Apple TV+, Hulu+, and several others. If you were to try to reach every one of those platforms, you could spend a lot of advertising dollars with each one. Or you could advertise on one or two networks that air on all those platforms. For example, you can watch TBS or Comedy Central on all the major cable and streaming services. Though again, this can be very expensive.

But what if you owned the content? What if instead of running a thirty-second spot in someone else's show, you produced your own show? Think that is a crazy idea? Chip and Joanna Gaines from my hometown of Waco are perfect examples. Joanna started off writing a blog that got the attention of a television producer and led to the launch of "Fixer Upper" on HGTV. That little show on cable grew the Gaines' small family business into an enterprise. Now you can buy their products at Target, and Chip and Joanna now have their own streaming network. That is the ultimate in content marketing.

I know you are thinking that this is an extreme example. True, but I have helped businesses launch podcasts, radio shows, and TV shows my entire career. Trade secret: the cost per thirty seconds to produce your own show is cheaper than to advertise in someone else's show. That local investment show hosted by someone who would love to help you with your investments? Yep, that is content marketing. The local car show hosted by someone who happens to know cars? You guessed it, content marketing.

But there are other forms of content marketing besides hosting a show. Writing a weekly blog can boost your business in several ways. Recording a weekly or daily video posted on social media can help you build a loyal following.

The secret sauce to content marketing is both owning the content and establishing yourself as the expert in your field. Content marketing can also be entertaining, and we will discuss some examples later in the book.

Does content marketing work? Yes. In the summer of 2020 in the height of the COVID-19 pandemic, my VP of Marketing called me out as a CEO. He said, "Scott, we are not practicing what we preach." That got my attention. Often as leaders we focus on helping our clients succeed, but we don't focus on doing the same for our own company. For years I had been telling CEOs and business leaders that they need to be the face of the company. They need to make appearances on TV, host a podcast, write a weekly blog, and post on social media on a regular basis. Yet I was not doing any of that for Centerpost Media, and we own two TV networks and a radio network!

Our company was growing, but we were not yet to profitability. We were still relying on investor money and vendor partners to keep up with the demands of the growth.

So, in January of 2021, I launched a weekly radio show and podcast called *Create. Build. Manage.* The focus was to create content that entrepreneurs and small business owners could use to grow their own business. We covered topics like closing more sales and tips on marketing, and interviewed successful leaders about their stories and what they learned when growing their business.

I started a video series on my social media called "People Over Profit," or POP for short, where I interviewed my staff and some clients to put the focus on them. They showed how we as a business were more focused on our people and our clients rather than profits.

I took my radio show to TV in October of 2021, airing it in more than twenty-five markets across the US.

The results? I have prospective clients coming to me asking for help. I have a PR Agent now and my publisher reached out and asked if I would write this book. Did I mention we are turning a profit?

I am a man of faith, so I give God all the glory for His blessings. He brings the rain, and He causes the growth. But it is our job to work the land and plant the seeds. Content marketing is planting the seeds for future growth. It is about keeping your brand front and center to your prospects, who may not be your prospects today but will remember you when they need your product or service.

Our vision statement at Centerpost Media is to help every business we encounter with their media needs by providing outstanding quality, service, and value. Our mission statement is that we want every business to grow as a result of our efforts, using content creation and distribution on television, radio, podcasts, websites, social media, and digital marketing. My prayer is that this book will accomplish both our vision and mission statements.

So buckle up and get ready to learn all you ever wanted to know and more about the history and trends of media. And get ready to pick up a few tips to get you started on content creation.

2

WRITTEN MEDIA

The Written Word is Powerful

INDIANA ATTORNEY ROGER BRANIGIN famously told a conference of 600 listeners in 1955, "I never argue with a man who buys ink by the barrel." In other words, Mr. Branigin felt fighting the newspaper publishers was a losing battle. Ten years later he became Indiana's Governor.

There is power in the written word. Throughout history we see examples of governments trying to censor what people can print. According to the Beacon for Freedom of Expression, the term "censor" can be traced back to the office of censor that the Roman government established in 443 BC.

But even before the official office of censor was established, people were so upset at Socrates for "corrupting the youth of his day," that they sentenced him to drink poison in 399 BC. Imagine a time where being a writer could get you sentenced to death. Unfortunately that still happens today in some parts of the world.

But what is so powerful about the written word? It is long lasting. This book will outlive me, which is a crazy thought. When you write something down you are putting it out there for others to read, form opinions, and share thoughts.

I am reminded of actor Yul Brynner's line from the movie "The Ten Commandments," where he played Pharaoh Ramesses: "So let it be written, so let it be done."

In addition to longevity, the written word gives the author the chance to fully flesh out his or her thoughts without interruption. Think about those times when you are trying to express how you feel or what you think about a topic with a friend or loved one. Often before you can fully process your thoughts or express your opinion, the other person jumps in with their thoughts or opinions. But have you ever written a letter to a friend or loved one? Not a text message or a quick email. I am talking about pen and paper and writing a letter.

As I mentioned earlier, I am a dad of two teenage daughters. I love my girls. Every now and again I will take time to write them a note to let them know how proud I am of them and how much I love them. I also make it a point to tell them every day the same, but the written letter has so much more meaning. To this day my youngest has a birthday letter I wrote her framed and hanging on her wall next to her mirror. The written word is powerful.

The Authority of Books

According to *Publishers Weekly*, print book sales rose 8.2% in 2020 from the previous year. More than 750.9 million units sold in the year ending on January 2, 2021. BookScan reports it was the largest annual increase since 2010. The pandemic, with kids learning at home, was cited as the main reason for the big jump in sales. But it was not just sheltering in place that led to an increase in book sales. According to Statista, there has been a steady climb in book sales since 2012, with only a slight decrease reported in 2019 before the boom in 2020.

If you want to research or learn about a topic, you turn to written material. Think back to your years in grade school or college or if you attended grad school. How many textbooks did you read? How many times did your teacher or professor assign additional reading material?

I love to read books. My favorite books are autobiographies and business books. I am a firm believer in further educating myself every year. When I read about other people's stories it gives me insight into what that author has learned on their journey through life. When Phil Knight wrote his book *Shoe Dog: A Memoir by the Creator of Nike*, it encouraged me as a business owner that even the founder of Nike had dark days where he thought his business would not make it, and yet he pressed on.

Business books give me tips on how I can be a better CEO. Sometimes I read about specific topics like sales so I can help my team get better at closing deals. Or I read other people's books on marketing to learn from their expertise.

When it comes time to choose who I will vote for in the presidential primaries, I like to read the books that the candidates have written to get an idea on who they are and where they want to lead our nation. Political speeches and cable news networks don't give you the full story like the candidate's book.

Books also help broaden the mind and see things from a different perspective. In the aftermath of the killing of George Floyd, TV Sports Analyst and former NFL linebacker Emmanuel Acho started a video series called "Uncomfortable Conversations with a Black Man." In November of 2020, he published a book of the same title. His work helped me start to see the racial injustices that still exist in our world today.

When you write something down, you also want to make sure you have all of your facts right. This book was written by me, but fact-checked by my assistant, my publisher, and a team of people. Why? Because like I mentioned, the written word lasts forever and is very powerful.

You can use a book to help market your business. I know the biggest hurdle in running a content marketing agency is knowledge. Most of our prospective clients don't know what they don't know, meaning they don't understand the power of content marketing. Creating content can change the course of their business, build a pipeline of prospective clients, and keep their current clients coming back for more products and services.

When I was approached about writing a book I jumped at the opportunity. Writing this book gives me an outlet to educate prospective and current clients on the changing landscape of media and how content marketing can help them. I can literally tell prospective clients that we wrote the book on content marketing.

On my radio show I have interviewed several authors who have taken the same path. Bob Tiede serves on the US Leadership Development team at CRU (Campus Crusade for Christ International in the US). His job is to recruit outstanding leaders from business, education, government, and medicine to mentor future leaders. He has written several books geared toward topics that help leaders. He does something amazing; he actually gives his books away for free. When I asked him why, he told me his desire is not to monetize from his work, but to be a resource to help others.

CRU is a non-profit ministry. Bob uses the books to build a relationship with future mentors. That is content marketing.

Curtis Morley is the Founder and CEO of *The Entrepreneur's Paradox*. He coaches other entrepreneurs, helping them learn from his mistakes when starting a business. He wrote the book on the subject. The Entrepreneur's Paradox discusses the sixteen pitfalls along the start-up journey. Morley's book establishes him as the expert and brings him new clients. That is content marketing.

Idan Shpizear is the founder of 911 Restoration, a company that helps people clean up after a disaster hits their home or business. He started to franchise his concept and wrote a book titled *Get Out of The Truck*, educating others on how to make more money running a trade business than being the person who does the work. What better way to start a business than to reach out to the guy who wrote the book and become a franchisee of 911 Restoration? That is content marketing.

If you are considering writing a book, I recommend you work with a publisher. They are the experts in this field and can help you throughout your process. A publisher has the same goal in mind as you do. They want the book to be a success. They will help you with your outline, copy edit your content, and give you helpful tips along the way. It can be a painful process at times, but you will have a better book working with a publisher.

You can self-publish a book, but I would not recommend that path. Unless you are a seasoned writer it is always best to work with someone who has experience working with authors.

Some words of advice: writing a book isn't just another day at the office. This is my first book, so the first thing I did was research how long this book should be. What I found is that a 200-page book is good for first time authors. This gave me a guide of how much information I should include. Part of that is how my brain works. I like a systematic process.

I also scheduled out my writing time to help me stay on track with the publishing deadline. This is important; if you don't block off time to write you will never write. And be prepared for all kinds of interruptions once you set aside time to write your book. I told my assistant to block off Fridays for writing. I am amazed how many people have since reached out and requested a meeting on Fridays. My first Friday I closed my office door and got in the zone. That same day our office had an AC company visit to add more cool air to our radio studio, and an electrician was onsite to upgrade a light outside my back-office door. Then our IT company showed up to update the computers. I use a noise canceling machine in my office. I highly recommend you purchase one to help block out outside noise.

This week my oldest surprised us by graduating high school early. The high school graduation is later this morning. Stay the course and keep writing! I am writing this section from my home office, so I got up early, drank some coffee, and got to writing so I could still make the graduation and stick to my timeline.

When writing, always start with an outline for your book. This helps you know where to start and where you are going. Again, your publisher can help you with this process.

You could also hire a ghostwriter to write your book. I am personally not a fan of this approach, because I believe you are the expert in your field. But if you are not a good writer, a ghostwriter will meet with you and interview you on your subject. This will still take time that you must budget. Time for the interviews and time to review the written material that has your name on it.

Newspapers are Not Dead

I KNOW SOCIETY likes to write-off different forms of media as being dead or irrelevant. But that simply is not true. Media doesn't die, per se, it just reinvents itself. Take the newspaper as an example. A Pew Research study released in 2021 showed the weekday print circulation of newspapers decreased by 19 percent in 2020 compared to 2019. Sunday print circulation decreased by 14 percent. Yet the same study showed a 27 percent increase in weekday digital circulation and 26 percent increase in Sunday digital circulation.

People are not leaving newspapers; they are just moving over to the digital editions. This has proved challenging for the newspaper industry. When digital editions first were offered, most newspapers did not charge a fee for their online stories. But as print subscriptions decline and the online readers increase, there has been a shift to charging a subscriber fee.

From a business standpoint, you can still advertise in newspapers and most offer a print and digital package. In fact, the newspapers were the first mainstream media to get wise to the new world of digital marketing. They understand search engine optimization and how to deliver prospects to their advertisers.

Pew Research data shows that when you combine print and digital readers, there are 24.3 million readers nationally for weekday editions and 25.8 million for Sunday editions.

I live and work in Arlington, Texas, and read the online version of the *Fort Worth Star-Telegram*. I like to keep up with what is going on locally in the news and read the sports writers' take on my favorite teams. Embedded in each article are local advertisements.

Your local newspaper is a business, and it needs to cut expenses and increase revenue. The newspaper needs content. One option you could consider is offering to write a weekly column for the newspaper. A friend and mentor, Dr. Don Newbury, writes a humorous column that is syndicated in more than 200 newspapers. He doesn't get paid for the column, but that column helps him land more speaking engagements. That is a form of content marketing.

Content marketing is about credibility. When you write on a subject you are saying to the world that you are an expert on the topic. I know we live in a world where we have thousands of social media experts. That is a topic for another chapter. I am referring to people who write a newspaper column or blog on a particular topic. In Dr. Newbury's example he is writing a funny column because his brand is the "after dinner" speaker. The person you invite to speak at a dinner for entertainment.

If you look at your local newspaper, you will also find someone who writes a weekly column about cars, who just so happens to own a car dealership. You might find a column on home improvement from someone who is a general contractor. These are all forms of content marketing.

If you want to advertise in your local newspaper, you can schedule a call with a sales agent to discuss campaign options. Never purchase rate card prices, but also understand the newspaper is a business and needs to make money. The best deals are always a win for both parties. Ask for examples of successful campaigns and even references from other businesses. Make sure your ad has a clear call to action. Ask for demographics and make sure they can deliver the prospect you are trying to reach. Subscriber count is important, but I believe demographics are more important. A newspaper can have thousands of subscribers, but if the demographics don't match who you are trying to reach, you are wasting your marketing dollars.

If you want to start writing a weekly column, start with submitting a letter to the editor. Newspapers will publish articles from readers on various subjects every week. Stay clear of hot topic issues that could alienate your prospects. But if there is a trending story that you're an expert in, submit a letter. This gives you some practice on writing an article.

Then you can reach out and set up a meeting with the publisher of the newspaper. Be prepared for an expense. Remember newspapers are for-profit businesses and you are asking to use their credibility and distribution to increase your business. You might get a free column in the paper if the publisher sees your point of view as sellable. Always worth the ask.

Newsletters Educate and Inform

WHERE THE GOAL of a newspaper is to cover a wide variety of news and information, newsletters are written to a specific audience for the purpose of educating and informing the end user on a particular topic.

Publicly traded companies often publish newsletters to their shareholders on a quarterly basis to show business trends. The newsletter contains an article written by the CEO giving his or her take on the previous quarter and outlook on the upcoming quarter. The newsletter might also contain featured articles highlighting an employee or client. These types of newsletters will contain graphs on the financial numbers. On the surface this might not seem like a form of marketing, but the goal of publicly traded companies is to keep investors excited about the future of the business. The newsletter is marketing to current and potential shareholders.

Other forms of newsletters are meant to educate consumers while strengthening the business' brand. One of our clients is *Financial Issues with Dan Celia*, a daily TV and Radio show that discusses investing money from a faith-based perspective. Dan publishes a newsletter for members that helps them know what companies align with their beliefs when considering investment dollars. The members get the information they are seeking and the message is on brand with Financial Issues.

As I mentioned, one of the challenges we have in our business is educating our clients and prospective clients. We started a monthly newsletter for our members giving them tips on how they can market their business. Each month we feature an article with some practical tips, highlight a member's company, and promote our services.

We also have a monthly newsletter that we blast to viewers and listeners of our networks. Where our member newsletter is written from a business-to-business perspective, the network newsletters are written from a business-to-consumer perspective. We highlight different shows that air on our networks. We invite show hosts to write an article to help promote their content. We give our viewers and listeners a rundown of upcoming programming, like what movies we are showing the next month. This newsletter is designed to keep people interested in watching or listening to our channels.

A newsletter can be printed and mailed to a list of current or former clients, or it can be published online on your company's website or sent via an email blast. The idea is to keep your products and services front of mind to your current and prospective clients. That gentle reminder that you are still in business and can help people with their needs.

If you are going to start a newsletter, make sure you define who the audience is and the purpose of the newsletter. You will also need good graphics to make your newsletter visually appealing. If you don't have a graphic artist on staff, you can use crowdsourcing or pay for a service that includes photos. Always make sure you have the rights to reprint or republish images online. Never use copyrighted material without permission.

Magazines Are King of Niche

WHEN YOU THINK about a magazine, you probably think about a particular topic that interests you. The magazine industry was the first to perfect niche content. I am willing to bet you can find a magazine for just about any topic you can imagine.

Stroll over to the magazine section in a bookstore and see how many different topics are in print. Hunting, fishing, football, basket weaving, and the list goes on and on. But this is good for a national business looking to reach a certain demographic.

If you offer a service or product nationally and you know the demographic you are trying to reach, a magazine can be a good option for you. For example, if you own a product that is used by hunters, advertising in a hunting magazine makes sense for your business. Let's say your product is not specific to hunting, but market research shows that the same demographic that subscribes to hunting magazines also needs your product or service. Again, this would be a great option for you.

You can also start your own publication if you have enough content to fill a magazine. This is typically for larger organizations. Universities print a monthly or quarterly magazine that is sent to alumni and sometimes prospective alumni. The goal is to showcase all the good that is taking place on campus, to keep alumni engaged, making it easier to raise money.

Though let's not confuse a magazine with a catalog. A catalog is just a large book with pictures of the products a company sells. A useful resource if you are selling office supplies or other tangible products.

But a magazine is all about pushing out content that people want or need to read, using that publication to then drive business. One of our media partners is BIC Media. They publish the largest magazine geared toward the energy business, like oil and gas. BIC has other services their company offers, like helping top level executives in the energy sector find work. This is content marketing. In fact, if you want to learn how a business owner uses books and magazines to drive business, look up my friend Earl Heard. He is a brilliant content marketer.

If you are going to consider advertising in a magazine, you need to do your homework to see which publication best fits your brand. If you are a local company, there are some great local options for you to consider. I receive two local publications in my mail every month. I never subscribed to them, but because they are delivered to my house, I read them both every time they're delivered. This is a great option for local advertising.

Like newspapers, you want to ask for detailed information about the demographics. Most magazines will give you a reader count that is four to five times the number of magazines that are actually printed. This is industry standard. The logic is, on average, each magazine is read by four to five individuals. All of this information is audited, you just have to know what questions to ask. Make sure you understand the number of magazines that are printed and delivered versus the reader count of the magazine. This will give you a better idea of the reach of your advertisement.

You want to make sure your ad in the magazine is creative and catches the attention of the reader. Less is more when it comes to print ads. You don't want a copy that is so busy the reader just passes by without taking the time. The magazine will offer support in this area, but you can also use your own graphics team. Just make sure you get the correct specs and delivery method for your ad, so you don't miss the deadline.

Trade show magazines are another option to consider. This kind of magazine ad buy is less about subscriber count as it will only be printed and delivered during a trade show. This is a great option for standing out, but again you want to make sure your ad has a clear call to action. If your business has a booth, use the ad to offer something free if they stop by your booth and mention the ad. This is a great way to track the results and get prospects coming to your booth.

Make sure the trade show publications are delivered to the attendees' hotel rooms and are offered in magazine stands around the convention. The best ones in which to buy ads are the official publications that include the agenda for the trade show and a map of the exhibit floor.

If you are going to consider starting your own magazine, I recommend you start with an online edition only. The biggest cost to a magazine is the printing and delivery. An online publication saves you the cost of both. If you really want to have a hard copy magazine for your business, reach out to someone in the industry for tips on negotiating the cost of paper, ink, and mailing of the magazine. All three are negotiable if you know how to navigate the industry.

Email Campaigns

ACCORDING TO MAILCHIMP, the average open rate for emails across the board is 22.7 percent. But opening an email does not equate reading an email. When you dig further into the numbers, the average click rate is only 2.91 percent. So do email blasts work? Yes.

Don't let the low open rate or click rate scare you away from considering an email campaign. Like with all marketing options, the creative has more to do with the success of an email campaign than the delivery method alone.

I get an email from Harbor Freight Tools in my personal inbox each month that always gets my attention. They do a great job showing images of different products they have to offer. They have designed their email to make the consumer feel like they are walking down the aisles of a hardware store. I can smell the new tools now. Clearly, I am their demographic. And that is the point. People don't mind being marketed to when it is a product they need or enjoy. Just ask the rabid Apple or Android product fans.

I separated this section from the newsletters and blogs because I think there is more to unpack when discussing email blasts. But it should be noted that you can use email blasts to send out your newsletter or blog. In fact, you can use an email blast to push people to all forms of digital marketing. Remember my Yahoo example. Yahoo emails me daily to promote their Yahoo news.

If you are going to consider an email blast as part of your marketing strategy, make sure the people receiving the email have opted in, otherwise you just become a spam marketer. There are no laws against spam per say, but you need to be careful. You also need to give people a clear and easy way to opt out of your emails. While you want to build as many subscribers to your email list as possible, you don't want to send emails to people who are not happy to receive them. That does not help you market your business.

Have a planned-out strategy with your email campaign. What is the call to action? What is going to get the prospect's attention? What are you promoting? It sounds simple enough but think of emails as cold calls. You are disrupting someone's day with an ask. Make sure that that ask is clear and to the point.

Some things to consider with email campaigns. Everything is trackable. You can see if the prospect opens the email and there are even sophisticated tools where you can see what the end user is clicking on in the email. If you didn't know it already, the companies sending you emails are tracking what you click on in the email. This helps the business learn what products or services you are interested in.

If this creeps you out to the point that you never want to open an email again, I have a consumer tip for you. Go to the email client you use on your computer or cell phone and turn off the option where your email automatically downloads the images. Those images are where the tracking devices are hidden.

We send email blasts to radio stations to consider picking up programs we syndicate through BizTalkRadio. We get reports on which shows the program directors click on and then we send follow-up emails and call the station to provide additional information on the show they have shown interest in picking up. It works! My radio affiliate team continues to add radio stations.

Pay close attention to who is not opening your emails. If that number is increasing it might be time to change the look of the blast. Over time, if the end user is not opening your email, your blast ends up in their junk folder. Outlook and Gmail, I'm looking at you.

Did you know you can make money from your email list? I am not talking about selling those lists to a third-party. See my note about spam emails. But other companies will pay to have their product featured in your newsletter if you have a healthy email list. Depending on your business, that could be an additional revenue stream.

I recommend working with a company that can help create and manage your email blast. A professional email marketer can make sure you are maximizing your creativity to get the most out of your marketing dollars.

Blogs Are the Most Affordable

NOTRE DAME OF Maryland University did an extensive study on blogs and concluded that Justin Hall created the first blog at Links.net in 1994. Hall wrote about HTML examples he found online. He did not call it a blog but referred to the site as his personal web page.

The term "weblog" was coined by Jorn Barger in 1997 to describe his quest of "logging the web." And in 1999 Peter Morholz shortened "weblog" to "blog." Today there are millions of blogs found online.

Blogging is the most affordable type of content marketing. You are literally just writing a short article and posting it on your website. But what do you write about and how often should you be posting to a blog?

The key to any content marketing is frequency and consistency. If you are going to start a blog, you need to be prepared to write a fresh article every week. Why? Because you want to build a loyal following of readers to have the greatest effect. You want the content to be fresh, not dated. If prospects come to your website and find a blog that was dated three years ago, that sends the message that you are not current. That your business is outdated. But if the same prospect sees fresh content on your website every week it makes your website look active and shows momentum.

Make your blog personal. People do business with people, not companies. I understand that is harder to prove with large corporations like Coca-Cola. People do not buy Coke because they like the CEO. Chances are most of us don't know who the CEO of Coke is. (It's James Quincey, but I cheated and Googled it.)

Chances are if you're reading this book, you are an entrepreneur or small business owner. You build your business through your reputation, and a blog is a great way for your clients and prospective clients to get to know you.

When I say personal, I am not suggesting you write about your family or favorite hobby and never discuss work. That does not make sense for a business blog. I simply mean don't be afraid to let your personality come through.

Much like this book, in my blog I mention my family and small personal tidbits about my life. It helps the reader get to know me and feel some connection with me. I use personal stories to tie into my topic.

For example, I wrote a blog about how content marketing is more effective than just cold calling. I told a story of when I was in my twenties and answered a classified ad for a marketing position. The job turned out to be a door-to-door position pushing a water delivery service. My "interview" was being paired with four other candidates to follow a sales expert and start making cold calls. Hours out on the streets and not a single sale. I described my personal pain of that story to relay how no one really likes cold calling. You can read my blog online at cenpostmedia.com.

You can write about your products and services, but you can also write on topics that the ideal customer would enjoy. Our prospects are business owners, so I often write about the things currently on the minds of business owners. Some examples include a blog I wrote on when to let someone go. Another blog was tips on how to stay motivated on a Monday when you miss the weekend. All the content is pushed out on social media and sent out via email to current, former, and prospective clients. The headlines need to be eye-catching and I recommend you use some great images as well to draw in the reader. When they click on the link it takes them to our website where we remind them of the services we have to offer.

In my case the blog also lets our prospects know that we understand what it is like to own and run a business, because we own and run a business.

Blogs also help your website get discovered. We will unpack search engine optimization more in Chapter Seven, but here's a quick preview: You need to keep your website fresh with new content each week to keep your website showing up in the top of the search engines. Blogs are a great way to add fresh content. Bonus when you use keywords to attract the right prospects.

Blogs are also a great way to educate the consumers on your products and services. You are the expert, and you can showcase your knowledge with a weekly blog.

But if you are going to consider writing a blog for your website, keep it short. You want the articles to be one page, maybe two. Too long and you will lose the reader. As mentioned before, make sure you are writing frequently and consistently. You also want to write with one voice. If you are going to invite several people on staff to contribute to the blog, you might consider running the articles by the same editor or laying out some standards to get everyone on the same page; or at the very least use the same layout each week and include bylines of which staff member is writing the blog.

One practical tip on keeping the blog consistent: I block off time on my calendar each week to blog. My calendar controls my day, so when it's time to write the blog I write the blog.

Looking for ideas for your next blog? Try matching the blog with the rest of your marketing efforts. Often my blog covers the same topic as my radio and TV show. Another good writing tip is to write what is on your mind. When I sit down and think about what I could write about, I often go to a place where my mind has already been processing information. The week I wrote about staying motivated on a Monday was when I needed to remind myself to stay engaged.

Conclusion

THE WRITTEN WORD in its many forms is still powerful. People still read books, newspapers, magazines, newsletters, and blogs.

If you are wanting to advertise alongside other people's works, study the demographics and reach out to find the right outlet to bring you prospects.

If you are looking to start your own written content creation, start with an online blog and work your way toward newsletters. Consider writing a column for your local newspaper. If your organization is large enough, you can look at starting a digital magazine. And when you are ready to write a book on your expertise, contact a publisher for support.

3

AUDIO MEDIA

Radio has always played an important role in my life. As a kid I would listen to the golden voice of the late Frank Fallon call the play-by-play of Baylor University games. I can still hear Frank's voice in my head at the end of a win, "This one belongs to the Baylor Bears."

When I was old enough to realize Mr. Fallon got paid to watch and talk about Baylor games, I knew what I wanted to do for a career. I spent more than a decade calling high school football games and some college, but being a professional sportscaster was not in the cards for me.

I also remember nights when I would tune into the local radio station to listen to music when I wanted to hear variety. This was before the Internet and music streaming, where there was only so much music I could actually own. I grew up in the age when record players and 8-tracks were phasing out and cassette tapes were popular, until our lives changed with CDs. Our family was one of the first in our neighborhood to get a CD player. To this day when I listen to the Oak Ridge Boys, Neil Diamond, or Julio Iglesias my mind goes back to my elementary years, listening to CDs and dancing on the fireplace hearth entertaining my parents.

I was captivated when a new radio station went on the air with a promotion advertising that "if you want one, mail us and we will send you one." They never said what the "one" was, but it turned out to be a bumper sticker. Brilliant marketing campaign.

Now it's the twenty-first century and I hardly ever tune in to the local radio stations. I catch myself listening to playlists I built on Spotify, or audio books or podcasts I have downloaded. When I want to catch up on Baylor sports, I listen to a streaming broadcast on the SICEM 365 App.

Is radio dead? No. Never trust a survey of one. People still tune into local radio and the medium is learning to reinvent itself.

History of Radio

THE SCIENCE BEHIND radio dates back as early as 1820 when Hans Christian Oersted studied electromagnetic waves. But according to PBS's American Experience, the early broadcasts were just a series of coded dots and dashes until Reginald Fessenden sent the first long-distance transmission of voice and music in 1906 from Brant Rock, Massachusetts, that was heard as far away as Norfolk, Virginia. Radio was born.

The golden age of radio is considered to be between the late 1920s until the early 1950s when America was introduced to television. But radio has survived with new inventions like FM frequencies that gave listeners a better quality of sound. Digital Audio Broadcasting not only transmitted digital quality of music over the public airwaves, but it also delivered visual displays on dashboards that let listeners know what song was playing or when the next traffic report was coming up.

Radio was the first form of mass media. Where print media, like newspapers, allowed for mass consumption of ideas, radio was the first to bring everyone together to listen to the ideas at the same time.

It's hard to imagine a time before information was available at the speed of light, but before the invention of radio it took days, weeks, and even years before news was known. Juneteenth is now a Federal Holiday, but it started as a day that Black Texans marked their freedom from slavery. As the Smithsonian describes, "Freedom finally came on June 19, 1865, when some 2,000 Union troops arrived in Galveston Bay, Texas. The army announced that the more than 250,000 enslaved black people in the state were free by executive decree. This day came to be known as 'Juneteenth,' by the newly freed people in Texas." This was two years after the executive decree was signed by President Abraham Lincoln. If commercial radio had been around in the 1860s, the news of their freedom would have been known the same day the decree was signed.

We Interrupt This Broadcast, is a book written by Joe Garner on the history of breaking news stories that the world learned about on radio and later TV. Garner gives a chronological history of the biggest news events. He starts with the Hindenburg explosion on May 6, 1937. Other major stories broke on radio, like the Pearl Harbor Attack, D-Day, and the dropping of the Atomic Bomb.

Because radio was the source for information, it also became the source for entertainment. Stars like George Burns and Gracie Allen got their start on radio. But who controlled the programming? The advertisers.

According to Britannica, "During American radio's Golden Age, much of the programming heard by listeners was controlled by advertising agencies, which conceived the shows, hired the talent and staff, and leased airtime and studio facilities from the radio networks." Content marketing was born.

The term "soap opera" comes from radio shows created and produced by soap companies. Market research showed that in the 1930s, the housewives controlled how money was spent on domestic products. During this era of the American family, housewives were at home all day and provided a captivated audience for radio stations. So the soap companies created radio dramas to keep the ladies listening all morning long, with mentions of the soap products peppered in throughout the broadcast. The very definition of content marketing.

As culture shifted in the United States, radio started tailoring its programming to "drive-time," which was during the morning drive to the office and the afternoon drive home. Local news, traffic and weather along with entertainment to get your day started and to help you unwind on the commute home.

Advertisers started sponsoring the segments people wanted to hear. Your traffic report was brought to you by a company. Of course, you had radio commercials in between the music or newscasts.

The Internet did not disrupt radio right away. In fact, radio actually embraced the Internet thanks in large part to websites like AudioNet. com, which was started by Todd Wagner and later funded by entrepreneur Mark Cuban. Best known today as the owner of the Dallas Mavericks, Cuban has long been a sports fan. Todd Wagner approached Mark with the idea of a website that broadcasts sports games from all over on one site. Cuban took majority control of the company and rebranded it Broadcast.com. In July of 1998, Broadcast.com went public, making Mark Cuban's net worth 300 million dollars. Cuban sold Broadcast.com to Yahoo for $5.7 billion in stock in 1999, and sold off his stock the same year netting him more than one billion cash; money he used to purchase an NBA franchise.

When I was in college in Brownwood, Texas, I worked for a local country radio station, KOXE. One day on the air I told a story about my parents. Nothing bad, just a funny story. I got a call from my mom that night asking me about the story. I responded, "Are you in town?" Nope, she heard me on Broadcast.com. Note to self, stop using your parents as an example. Oh wait—I guess some lessons are never learned!

Broadcast.com ended in 2002 when Yahoo needed to shut down the service to save money following the dot com bust.

Everything started to change for radio with the rollout of smart devices. Now you could listen to music on the go, but you had to plug your devices into an auxiliary port in your car. That is until car manufacturers began integrating the smartphones into the dashboards of vehicles. Now radio competes for attention from streamers and podcasters.

Traditional Radio Still Has Listeners

ACCORDING TO DATA released from Statista in July of 2021, radio reaches 82.5 percent of adults weekly in America. On average, Americans listened to ninety-nine minutes of radio per day in 2020, largely during their commute.

There are more than fifteen thousand commercial radio stations in the US that generate an estimated 21.6 billion dollars in annual revenue.

"Radio is the number-one reach medium, hands down," said Tammy Greenberg, Senior Vice President of Business Development at RAB (Radio Advertising Bureau). "Given what we've all collectively been through over the past eighteen months or so, people are experiencing extreme screen fatigue. And as a result of that, audio is what consumers are leaning into."

So again, is radio dead? Clearly it is not. Radio is still a viable option for business owners who want to get the word out about their products or services. "Radio is a connection to the local community," Greenberg said. "88 percent of radio listeners believe that radio's primary advantage is its local feel, and their connection with their home radio station is really key."

Let's discuss traditional advertising first. What should you consider if you want to advertise your business on radio?

Always start with demographics rather than the total number of listeners. Radio stations are rated by Nielsen Audio, formally known as Arbitron Inc. Nielsen is a powerful research group that measures radio stations using Portable People Meters. The PPMs are worn by respondents and pick up encoded audio signals. That data is collected and Nielsen then estimates how many people are listening to a particular radio station. They also compare demographic information from the respondents to build a profile of who listens to a radio station.

In smaller markets, Nielsen still sends out paper diaries, where the respondents fill out what radio station they are listening to. Again, Nielsen estimates the total listeners based on the data collected and the demographics based on who is reporting the data.

The purpose of ratings is to find an industry standard for advertising rate cards. If you think about it, radio stations are selling air. It's not like a product you purchase online or in a retail store. You cannot hold the product that radio stations sell you in your hands. To try to quantify the value of what a radio station offers a business, the ratings system was created.

Most business owners I meet know they need to ask about ratings, but they have no clue what the data means. So let me unpack ratings for you. According to Nielsen, stations are measured on the average quarter-hour. The idea behind this measurement is you will be in your car for at least fifteen minutes.

Nielsen Audio will provide data that shows the average quarter-hour persons (AQH PERSONS), which is the average number of persons listening to a radio station for at least five minutes of the fifteen minute period.

They also provide the average quarter-hour rating (AQH RATING), which is a math formula they use based on the percentage of the population that is being measured. In other words, how a particular radio station compares to the competition.

Then you get into the cost per rating point (CRP) and the cost per thousand (CPM). This is how much a radio station will charge you for reach.

Another number you will see is the CUME, short for cumulative audience. CUME is the total number of different persons who tune in to a radio station for at least five minutes during a particular part of the day. That leads to the CUME rating, which is the overall percentage of people estimated in a specific demographic group that listens to the radio station.

Insider tip: national advertisers will discount their buy based on the demographics they are trying to reach. If Brand X only wants to reach men aged eighteen through twenty-five, they will negotiate to pay for the ratings of those specified men, not the overall rating.

Confused yet? Bottom line, if you are going to purchase advertising off of ratings, make sure you understand what each term and number means.

But let's unpack the reality of ratings. They are not 100 percent accurate—how could they be? If you are listening to a radio station and are not near one of the Portable People Meters, does Nielsen know you are listening? No. Furthermore, how can they know the total number of listeners based on the sample they are collecting? They can't, which is why it is an estimated number.

This is why I am more interested in results rather than total numbers. Results are not estimated, they are facts. If you run a campaign on a local radio station and you see an uptick in your overall business, that is a fact. Radio is working for you. Conversely, if you are spending money on radio and not seeing results, radio is not working for you.

I know what you are thinking. Then how do I know if radio will work for my business before I make a purchase? Great question. Focus on demographics instead of number of listeners. Radio stations have different ways to track demographics. Yes, they still use Nielsen Audio, but they also see data from their website and if they have a radio station app. Generally speaking, the people who come to a radio station website are the same people who listen to that radio station. We will discuss how the digital world is very trackable later in this book, but Google Analytics is a great resource to study the radio station's demographics.

What does the profile of the listener who calls into the radio station look like? Most radio stations keep track of caller data to help them make decisions on programming. What does market research show about the format of the radio station? There is data available that shows what type of demographic listens to a particular format. Talk Radio, as an example, pulls in a larger male demographic. We own BizTalkRadio and we can track that we have an 80/20 male to female demographic with the average age over fifty-five.

The reason I believe demographics are key is because you want to match your product or service to the person you are trying to reach. If a radio station tells you that they have 100,000 listeners, but they are not reaching the demographic you need, why spend the marketing dollars on that station?

If you are going to test a radio station, be prepared to run your campaign for a minimum of thirteen weeks, but I would recommend twenty-six weeks. Radio advertising is all about frequency and consistency. It takes time for the listener to hear your spot, understand what you are offering, and respond to your advertisement. Most new businesses don't understand this truth and get impatient when their radio spot does not work after thirty days.

If you want some assurance that your business will work on a particular radio station, ask for success stories. Reach out to the businesses you hear advertising on the station themselves and ask them how long they ran their ads until they saw results.

The Growing Trend of Internet Radio

INTERNET RADIO IS a growing sector of the business, with iHeartRadio being the largest player with a reported 300,000 average active sessions. Americans listened to internet radio an estimated 974 minutes a month in 2021, according to Statista.

Internet radio is defined as a continuous stream you listen to online via your computer, smartphone, or streaming device. Typically, internet radio is described as a 24/7 stream that is delivered via the internet instead of your radio antenna. Streaming services like Apple Music and Podcasting are considered their own category.

Most of your internet radio stations are traditional radio stations that stream their content. Much like a newspaper offering its articles online, radio stations stream their content on their website and through an app you can download to your smartphone.

Remember all digital content can be tracked, so there is no guess-work when it comes to online listener data. I mentioned we owned BizTalkRadio—well we have an app you can download to your phone. We can track data that shows how many people have downloaded our phone app and what device they downloaded it to; be it Android, iPhone, or BlackBerry. We can also track how many unique listeners are tuning in to the stream and where they are located in the world.

From a consumer standpoint this might sound creepy, but it is the reality of living in a digital space. Every time you open an app on your phone, the creator of the app knows you are interacting with their content, the approximate location of your device, and some basic demographic information about you. Scary, I know, but true.

To be clear, there is a lot of information that can be tracked but is not shared with third-party companies like radio stations. The phone networks probably know more about you than you know about yourself, and I am guessing so do the phone manufacturers. Think about it—the phone companies maintain the cell phone towers and they know your exact location. Ever use an app like "Find a Friend?" Well, your carrier can "find a customer." This is true with both Apple and Android phones.

We will get more into digital tracking later in this book, but I wanted to set the record straight that personal information like your name, home address, and work address are not passed on to internet radio stations. But they do know when someone is listening to their stream and they know what city they are listening from, and based on that data they can guess your demographic. It has to do with public information provided by the US Census Bureau.

All of this to say, ask for detailed information when considering advertising on an internet radio station. They might protect some information, but they can give you a profile of who is listening and how often.

If you are advertising on a local radio station's stream, the demographics will be similar to the over-the-air listeners. There are internet-only radio stations, where someone has started a service online but they do not own a traditional radio station. I have a friend who used to work in radio, but over the years started a large collection of records. He has since digitized the records and launched several internet-only radio stations. He uses his feeds to broadcast local sports and even does live remotes. But the only way to listen to his station is online. You can advertise on these types of stations as well. Just follow the data and ask who is listening.

Streaming On-Demand Content

STATISTA DATA FROM 2018 and 2019 shows that Apple Music is the most listened-to streaming service, followed by Spotify, Pandora Radio, and iHeartRadio.

Streaming services are different from internet radio, in that they offer the consumer the option to either skip a song they don't like or even build their own playlist. Most of the streaming services offer a free version with commercials and a premium commercial-free version.

From an advertising perspective, the ad-free premium streaming services are a non-starter. There is not a way for you to market your business on the premium services. As these platforms grow, educate yourself and your team on other forms of marketing. Much like DVRs in television, on-demand commercial-free music does not give the advertiser options to promote products.

On the other hand, the ad supported streaming services are perfect for local businesses who want to reach a certain demographic or geo-targeted area.

Because streaming devices ping off of cell phone towers when mobile or can be tracked to IP addresses when listened to at home, advertising can be geo-targeted to a particular location. The same is true for some of the large radio station groups that have their own apps.

If you own a local restaurant and your research shows your target customer will drive up to twenty miles to eat at your establishment, you can buy ads on the streaming platforms that only cover your area. I live in the Dallas-Fort Worth Metroplex, which is like having several large pockets under the same DMA. I specifically live in Arlington, so when we eat out at a restaurant it is most likely going to be in the Arlington area of the Metroplex. When I listen to Pandora, I hear ads for car dealerships and other businesses located in Arlington. In this sense, it is a better use of your marketing dollars if you are hyper-local.

Satellite Radio Has Its Place

I USED TO program a channel for SIRIUS Satellite Radio before it merged with XM. It was during a season when satellite radio was the new shiny object. The concept also rolled out before smartphones were readily accessible via the dashboards of vehicles. If you wanted to be able to listen to the same station from coast to coast, satellite radio was the best option.

Remember road trips as a kid? Driving town to town and trying to find a radio station to listen to along the way. In 1983, my family moved from Waco to Odessa where my dad's job took him for a couple of years before we moved back home. Even though the song came out in 1980, it seems like we heard Willie Nelson sing "On the Road Again" a million times on the seven hour road trip.

In 2005, when I was hired to build FamilyNet Radio, I was given a couple of after-market satellite radios. In 2007, FamilyNet was purchased by In Touch Ministries in Atlanta, which meant my family packed up and moved out of state. Most of our family is from and lives in Texas. Every Christmas we loaded up the minivan and headed west for a couple of weeks. We loved listening to the different channels, sports, and news we got on SIRIUS radio.

But I noticed some obvious trends from a marketing standpoint. The majority of listeners to our channel were truck drivers or sports fans. Truck drivers are always on the road, and satellite radio was a great option for them. And sports fans liked the fact that they could listen to every NFL and most major college games.

Understanding that trend, I launched an overnight live call-in show that helped listeners who were lonely. June Hunt's "Hope in the Night" program was not new, but a perfect show for our channel. Ms. Hunt loved interacting with the truck drivers who just needed to talk to a friendly voice. We also had an original morning show that encouraged truck drivers to call in. A popular segment was "Thankful Thursdays," when people just called to say what they were thankful about.

Part of our deal with SIRIUS was that they could preempt our channel on Saturdays for college football. As a faith-based channel it became problematic when SIRIUS aired football broadcasts that included beer advertisements. Being from Waco and counting John Morris (the voice of the Baylor Bears) as a friend, I also negotiated a deal to be the official channel on SIRIUS to air Baylor athletics. Baylor is a Baptist school and we were a Baptist channel.

I am sure the demographics have expanded beyond truck drivers and sports fans today. According to SIRIUS XM, they have sixty-nine million people who are listening weekly to satellite radio. If you are looking to advertise nationally, satellite is an option to explore. I would ask for details on the number of actual listeners and demographics.

Don't get caught up in subscriber numbers with satellite radio, as that number can be very misleading. Subscribers are counted as every vehicle that currently has satellite radio activated. That can include the unsold cars that have a demo active for prospects to tune in to on test drives. When you buy a new or used car today, it often comes with three months free of satellite radio. I purchased a used car this year and tuned in twice to satellite radio. Personally, I think internet radio or streaming from your phone sounds better than satellite radio that has a limited bandwidth to deliver all those channels to you.

Podcasts Are Hot

WELCOME TO THE new age of talk radio: podcasts. But the concept of a podcast is not that new. Some argue its roots go as far back as the 1980s when those rad dudes were "audio-blogging." Cowabunga!

A podcast is simply an audio file that you can download and listen to on-demand.

Podcasting started to take off around the same time that smartphones were integrated into the dashboard of vehicles, making it easier than ever for listeners to consume their favorite podcasts.

According to Insider Intelligence, the largest destinations for podcast listeners are Apple Podcast, YouTube, and Spotify. Spotify is projected to pass Apple Podcast with 28.2 million US internet users a month compared to twenty-eight million on Apple in 2021.

Overall, the estimated US podcast listeners increased by 10.1 percent in 2021 to 117.8 million. That is a lot of downloads. The biggest growth is in the younger demographics, with 60 percent of adults ages eighteen through thirty-four listening to podcasts monthly.

You can advertise on a podcast much in the same way you would advertise on a radio show. Contact the podcast with which you are interested in advertising; discuss reach and demographics and what options are available to purchase. Live reads are popular in traditional talk radio and popular in podcasts. These are endorsement deals where the host of the podcast or radio show will endorse your product or service. "It's part of what they do," Greenberg said. "They use the product and they are listeners' friends, they are their trusted reliable source. So, when it comes to word-of-mouth, there is nothing better than a radio personality endorsing a brand because they're the ones that are driving the word-of-mouth."

Audio Programmatic Advertising

PROGRAMMATIC ADVERTISING IS a concept that I will introduce in this chapter but talk about in greater detail in Chapter Six when looking at OTT advertising, and in Chapter Nine we will discuss the different types of Programmatic when we dive into digital advertising. Programmatic Advertising is sometimes called programmatic marketing, programmatic media, or programmatic programming.

Imagine a live auction to purchase commercial inventory. Picture a room of advertisers who are all bidding for placement of their commercial spot, right up to the seconds before that spot airs. That is Programmatic Advertising. But instead of an actual room with humans, the room is filled with artificial intelligence and powered by algorithms to evaluate consumers based on their behaviors, demographic data, internet cookies, and additional information to decide what type of commercial should be aired, and then matching that consumer with the perfect advertiser.

In the world of podcasting, Programmatic Advertising takes keywords from the podcasts and matches up with potential advertisers in addition to tracking the consumer. For example, when you are listening to my podcast *Create. Build. Manage.* you might hear a commercial for an insurance salesperson in your city. Chances are you own a business, and you might be shopping for insurance.

Think of it this way—in the traditional sense, as an advertiser you don't know when or where a consumer will listen to a particular podcast. But you do know what demographic you are trying to reach. Programmatic Advertising allows you to set a budget and the AI will find your demographic and play your ad, giving you the impressions you want to reach.

You can also purchase Programmatic audio ads in audio streaming services.

According to ToolBox Marketing, the major players in the Programmatic audio space are Google, SoundCloud, Pandora, BBC, and Rubicon Project.

Audio Content Marketing

RATHER THAN GIVE you specific examples of content marketing in each audio category, I wanted to write about it separately, because audio content marketing is the same whether you are talking about radio, satellite radio, internet radio, streaming, or a podcast.

Remember, traditional advertising is renting space on someone else's platform to market your product or service. Content marketing is creating your own platform to build a following of current and prospective clients or customers.

When you host your own audio show, you are the expert. You set the agenda for the show, and you can use the platform to build a massive pipeline of business. For example, if you own a home repair business, you could create a show (radio, on satellite, online, streaming, or podcast) demonstrating simple repairs. The show attracts homeowners interested in the content. When the homeowner runs into a project too big for their skillset, they will remember your business and reach out for help.

You can also use the audio content on social media. More tips on how in Chapter Eight.

This type of content marketing creates both direct and indirect results. Direct results are from the listeners who find your show on the radio or start subscribing to your podcast. Indirect is when you create the "cocktail napkin" marketing for your business. This is when you are at a party and someone asks you what you do for a living. Rather than tell them you own a home repair business, tell them you host a radio show on how to do simple repairs around the house. Media is powerful and people want to hear about your radio show. Most consumers don't understand that to get a radio show all you have to do is purchase time at the local radio station, or if you are national, you purchase time through a syndicator like BizTalkRadio. Of course, you understand this concept because you are reading this book!

I have worked in media my entire career, but I'm naturally an introverted person. Before I understood the power of networking and content marketing, I always wanted to hide in the back of a room in social settings. When people asked me what I did for a living, I stopped telling them I worked in media. Telling a stranger that I worked in media led to a list of questions they wanted answered. People are fascinated with media. I started telling people I worked in communications, and I guess they thought I worked for the phone company, but they never asked and moved on. By the way, I am way more social today, but my point is that media is very powerful and content marketing goes beyond the direct results you get on the platform.

My friend Gary Leland is one of the founders of the Podcast Movement, the largest convention for podcasters. Gary is an entrepreneur, not a professional broadcaster. But I would be willing to bet he has made more money from audio content marketing than most people who studied broadcasting in school. Leland learned early on that a podcast aggregates the prospects you are trying to reach. He owned a softball equipment business and started a fast-pitch softball podcast. The content discussed the game to draw in the listeners, and his business sponsored the podcast to close sales.

Gary also owned a wallpaper business with his wife Kathy. A podcast on wallpaper would be rather boring to listen to, so instead he created a podcast talking about the latest episode of "Fixer Upper" that aired on HGTV. Brilliant. Several fans of the TV show tuned in each week to hear more about the show, and it was sponsored by his wallpaper company.

Notice a trend? When you are creating audio content you are not creating a longer commercial. The clients that fail at content marketing are the ones that want to spend the entire show talking about their business. No one wants to subscribe to an infomercial. If you are looking to start a podcast or a radio show, you want to create content that people are interested in.

For my show, *Create. Build. Manage.*, I don't talk about content marketing the entire hour. Instead, I discuss topics that business owners and entrepreneurs are interested in, and I have built an audience of prospects who know that if they need help with content marketing, they can reach out to me.

Conclusion

PEOPLE LISTEN TO audio on the go, so spending marketing dollars on the audio medium is money well spent. Think of the hours Americans spend in their vehicle driving to work, picking up their kids, and traveling on vacation. They want to be informed and entertained. They are a captivated audience. Like all forms of marketing, do your research and ask informed questions.

Audio media is the most personal form of media in my view. It is like having a conversation with the listener. You have to make time to sit down and read or pick up the remote and watch TV, but your car stereo is always on when you turn on the engine.

Keep that in mind if you go the route of advertising on any audio platform. Make your commercial reads personal. Same if you decide to start your own show—talk to one person. That is the first piece of advice I give any new show host. When you talk into the mic, imagine you are talking to one person. It makes the listener feel special.

4

VIDEO MEDIA

I AM OLD enough to remember life before there were endless options for watching content. Cable TV was invented before I was born, but it exploded in the 1980s. Our family went from a small television where us kids were the remote control, dad telling us to get up and change the channel, to a large piece of furniture made by Zenith.

We watched shows like *Little House on the Prairie*, *The Dukes of Hazzard*, and *Knight Rider*. I would sneak into the living room late on Saturday nights to try to figure out why my parents were laughing watching *Saturday Night Live*.

When I got home from school, sometimes mom would let me watch a cartoon before starting my homework. Other times I had to get all my homework finished before I could turn on the TV. When dad got home from work, it was the nightly news followed by *Wheel of Fortune*.

We were one of those families that had the TV on during dinner, watching shows like *Alf* and *Family Ties*.

Saturday mornings were my favorite. I would wake up early to watch cartoons like *Garfield and Friends*, and *Muppet Babies*. As I got older, I never missed an episode of *Saved by The Bell*. What pre-teen boy did not have a crush on Kelly Kapowski, played by Tiffani Amber Thiessen?

I remember walking into a video rental store and seeing rows and rows of movies to rent. Our family did not own a VCR, so we used to rent one from the store. Friday nights became movie nights as we watched films like *Back to The Future*, *The Karate Kid*, and *Batman*. When I was in third grade my parents told me if I learned my multiplication tables, they would reward me with a surprise. The surprise was, they bought the family a VCR. Thanks math.

The Disney Channel was a premium offering that my parents paid the extra money for every month. Endless hours of classic movies, cartoons, and features of the new rides at the Disney theme parks. Then there was the reboot of *The Mickey Mouse Club*, with stars like Britney Spears, Justin Timberlake, and Christina Aguilera.

As I got older, I was more interested in sports, watching the Raycom game of the week, Monday Night Football, and hours upon hours of baseball games.

My wife and I first connected in college over the TV show, *The West Wing*. She would come over to my house and we would watch an episode together and talk about the series. We were both communication majors and loved how well written the show was and how fast paced the dialog.

When we got married, we had a VHS tape for each night of the week and would catch up on our shows on the weekend. When the DVR was introduced and our kids were still young, we would put them down for the night on Fridays and I would have my laptop open catching up on emails as we watched shows together.

When our girls were growing up our TV was tuned into *Dora the Explorer*, *The Mickey Mouse Clubhouse*, and still my wife's favorite, *Phineas and Ferb*.

TV is a part of the American experience. Each show represents a season in life. Popular shows become conversations at the office. The nation wanted to know who shot JR on the primetime soap *Dallas* in

1980. More than 100 million Americans tuned in to the final episode of *M*A*S*H** in 1983.

And we all watched major events unfold live on TV, like when the Space Shuttle Challenger exploded or the events of 9/11, when we saw the second plane hit the World Trade Tower and knew our nation was under attack.

Video is powerful and will continue to be powerful. Nothing conveys a message better than with video, and businesses have been learning to use video to tell their story on television and in the new platforms that continue to evolve.

The History of Television

PHILO FARNSWORTH INVENTED the video camera tube, the image dissector, and the first fully functional all-electronic television system in 1927.

The camera tubes allowed television cameras to capture video images. The tube technology was used widely until the 1980s and as late as the 1990s. The image dissector, also known as a dissector tube, created an electron image that was scanned to produce an electrical signal that represented a visual image. The dissector was replaced with newer tube technology in the 1930s called an iconoscope. The iconoscope was invented by Vladimir Zworykin, who worked for Radio Corporation of America (RCA).

That led to a legal battle between Farnsworth and RCA over who owned the rights to sell the technology. In the end, RCA agreed to pay Farnsworth a multi-year licensing agreement for use of his patent, totaling $1 million. RCA was now the leader in the industry and introduced the world to commercial television at New York's World's Fair in 1939.

The Berlin Olympic Games were the first to be televised using the new RCA equipment. The BBC broadcast the coronation of King George VI and Wimbledon in the late 1930s to 9,000 television sets.

On July 1, 1941, the Federal Communications Commission (FCC) authorized commercial broadcasting. The attack on Pearl Harbor was the first major news event to be covered on TV, but there were not that many TV sets sold at that time, and most were in the New York area.

Manufacturing of TV sets came to a halt during World War II when the US government banned factories from producing televisions and converted assembly lines to crank out military equipment to win the war. Most research was also focused on war efforts, but the invention of radar led to improvements in television design.

Post war, television started to become a part of Americana, with the broadcasting of the World Series in 1947. *Howdy Doody* was the first children's program that debuted on December 29, 1947, on NBC.

By the late 1940s, there were two million TV sets in the marketplace, but most were still in the New York DMA. By 1951, there were thirteen million television sets when President Truman became the first coast-to-coast telecaster when he addressed the nation.

In 1954, RCA introduced the first color television set, but it took a decade before NBC would start airing prime time shows in color.

Cable television took off in the 1980s and introduced the public to pay-service-cable channels like Home Box Office (HBO). Now America had thirty channels to watch, not just three channels. Of course, that quickly exploded to hundreds of channels.

In December of 1996, WCBS in New York was the first station to broadcast in High-Definition. The early HD technology broadcast in a 720p resolution. Resolution is the number of pixels displayed on the screen. The higher the pixel count, the sharper the image. Before HD the resolution was 480i. Shortly after 720p was introduced, 1080p became commercially available. Today 4k TVs are sold which can have a resolution up to 2160p. And higher resolution TVs are being tested in other markets today.

Broadcast TV, What's Old is New Again

BROADCAST TV IS defined as television broadcast over the public airwaves. An industry term used is Over-the-Air, or OTA for short. Before paid cable TV and way before the internet was invented, antennas were the only means to watch television.

The technology used radio waves to send analog signals over-the-air, broadcast on a specific frequency. Antennas in the home would intercept the analog waves and convert them to tiny radio frequency alternating currents, which were then applied to the TV's tuner to extract the television signal.

TV channels were broadcasted on either VHF bands, which is a high frequency of channels two through thirteen, or UHF band, an even higher frequency of channels fourteen through fifty-one. You might be old enough to remember an antenna having two settings to toggle back and forth between VHF and UHF frequencies.

It is crazy to think about this, but even today there are frequencies all around you broadcasting TV and radio signals. Frequencies have also been used in shortwave radios, cordless phones, and your TV remote. The Federal Communications Commission (FCC) regulates all of the frequencies in the United States, which means the government actually owns the airwaves and licenses them for commercial use.

That means your local TV stations are subject to federal broadcasting standards. It is why you don't see nudity or hear four letter words on the major broadcasting stations. In 2007, Atlanta TV station WTBS changed its call letters to WPCH and rebranded the local channel to Peachtree TV. Prior to this change TBS on cable TV would just just rebroadcast WTBS, so the channel was subject to FCC over-the-air broadcast standards. Once they separated the two, TBS could air more adult content in the evenings, including unedited movies. Cable is not broadcast over the public airwaves. That is why you will occasionally see nudity, and more and more cable channels allow four letter words.

That is not to say the FCC doesn't have oversight for cable. When cable TV was rolling out in some parts of the country in the 1960s, the FCC passed a law requiring cable systems to carry certain broadcast channels. These channels are called "must-carry" stations.

According to Britannica, early programs on TV were mostly shows that were simulcast on radio. Major motion picture studios wanted little to do with the new medium. The videotape was not in widespread use until the 1960s, so broadcasters had to rely on live programming. This meant TV viewers watched live musical performances, sports, church services, and in-studio variety shows.

Sponsors played a major role in underwriting the shows. Often a live announcer would read the commercial advertisement, or the host would promote a product in the show.

Content marketing, where advertisers created entertainment programming to build an audience to promote their products, has a long-standing history with television. On the national level the soap companies took their dramas to TV.

Disney created a show that aired on ABC that promoted a new theme park. *The Wonderful World of Disney* was hosted by Walt Disney, who would show viewers what the park would look like before showing a made-for-TV movie or show on Sunday nights. It is a concept the company has continued to use, creating the Disney Channel and Disney XD, and Disney now owns ESPN and ABC. All those channels still promote the Disney brand and push people to their theme parks. You can stay at the ESPN Wide World of Sports complex in Orlando. And don't be surprised to see upcoming Disney movies promoted across all their channels.

Though it's not just Disney. Hallmark Cards started producing a program titled *Hallmark Television Playhouse* on NBC in December of 1951. It was a spinoff of their radio show *Hallmark Playhouse* that aired on CBS radio in the late 1940s. In 1953 they renamed the series *Hallmark Hall of Fame*. What started off as live plays became specials seen a few times a year. Hallmark started to produce made-for-TV movies that aired on CBS and later ABC. Today, Hallmark is the number-one cable channel in December when they air all made-for-TV Christmas movies. Crown Media also has Hallmark Movies & Mysteries and Hallmark Drama.

As a side note, when I first started working for FamilyNet TV, it was owned by the Southern Baptist Convention, who used to own a channel called ACTS (American Christian Television System). The SBC started to sell off shares of the channel to a larger faith group called Vision Interfaith Satellite Network (VISN.) The channel was rebranded Faith and Values Channel in 1993 and Liberty Media acquired 49 percent ownership in 1995. The channel was rebranded Odyssey in 1996. Hallmark and Jim Henson purchased shares in Odyssey in late 1998. Working with Liberty Media, Odyssey started using the tagline "a Hallmark and Henson Network." In 2001, it was rebranded Hallmark Channel.

Media really is a small business. The company I work for today owns the rights to some of the original content that aired on ACTS through a series of acquisitions, and my lead investor built the Regional Sports Networks and worked for Liberty Media during this season.

The Digital Transition and Public Safety Act of 2005 was passed, making it mandatory that all full power broadcast stations switch from analog to digital broadcasting by February 17, 2009. The DTV Delay Act changed the analog cutoff date to June 12, 2009, to give consumers more time to purchase a digital convertor box.

Under the old analog signal, there was a broadcast wave that took a set bandwidth to deliver over-the-air. The new digital signals opened the opportunity for broadcast stations to compress signals in the delivery to the TV sets. Thus, the digital sub-channels were created.

Digital sub-channels are the additional channels offered for free over-the-air. As an example, in Dallas, Channel 8 is the ABC affiliate. When tuning in via a broadcast antenna, you can watch 8.1, 8.2, 8.3— usually up to six sub-channels. DFW alone has more than 100 channels available for free with a digital antenna.

This led to the creation of Digi-Nets, networks that program specifically for the digital sub-channels. We own BizTV, one of the original Digi-Nets that was launched in August of 2009.

What is old is new again. Deloitte published an article in the Wall Street Journal that reported "more than 40 million Americans in at least 16 million homes watch antenna TV, up 48% since 2010."

This is a great opportunity for businesses that want to advertise their products or services. Antenna TV is live TV. There is no DVR. That means there are millions of potential customers watching free over-the-air TV. There is also a smaller number of channels compared to cable or the internet. More likely that your target demographic will see the commercial spot.

You can advertise on the major local channels and pay a premium rate for commercials. The pro is you would get both over-the-air and cable homes. The con is you are paying for cable homes where a growing number of viewers record content on a DVR and fast-forward through the commercials. If you are looking at this option, there are a few things to consider. Like radio, your local TV station relies on ratings to set the price point for commercials.

Nielson is looking at set top box data on all the major cable systems, advanced metering technology, and data collected from people to determine ratings. If you are watching cable, what you are watching is recorded live and shared with services like Nielson. They cross reference that data with publicly available demographic information and share their findings with the local stations for a price.

Ratings are percentages that measure demographics. A common example is adults eighteen through forty-nine that watch a particular show. One point is equal to 1.28 million viewers. So, if a particular show gets a rating of three in an age range, that means they have roughly 3.84 million people who tune in to watch that show.

Remember that ratings were created to try to quantify the media buy. It is a science, but not perfect. Like radio, Nielson cannot measure over-the-air viewing with the same level of scrutiny as cable TV. If you are watching TV over-the-air in your home off an antenna, that is impossible to fully measure. But Nielson is the industry standard because they have invested the resources to get as accurate a number as possible.

Where a rating is the number, a share is the percentage of the overall people in an age group that is watching a particular program. So, if you read that a show had an eight share in adults eighteen through forty-nine, that means that 80 percent of adults under fifty were watching that particular show.

Finally, total viewers are the total number of people tuned in to that show.

Buy off demographics, not total number of viewers. Who are you trying to reach? That is always more important when you look at buying any media. Match your product with the program. If you are selling a product that appeals to women over forty, but under sixty, do your research to spend advertising dollars in programs that are reaching that demographic.

Sponsoring local digital subchannels is a great option for a local business that wants to reach the growing number of viewers who are watching free, over-the-air TV. Because most digital sub-channels are broadcast only, the cost per spot is more affordable. Ratings information may be harder to obtain, but the channel should be able to give you demographic information based on third-party services like Google Analytics.

Remember, when it comes to running spots, it is all about frequency and consistency. It takes the average viewer seven to fourteen times before they will register what your commercial spot is about and respond to the call of action.

On the content marketing side, you can buy time on local stations to air your own content. Real Estate Agencies will often produce a local show to help sell houses. This is an expensive option if you are purchasing time on the local NBC, ABC, CBS, or FOX affiliate. But you can purchase time on one of the sub-channels. Use your social media to drive an audience and in turn use the fact you have a local TV show to drive more business. Remember the "cocktail napkin" marketing approach? Having your own TV show is the next step above having your own radio show.

Do you have a ton of content, and you want to take your marketing strategy to the next level? You can sub-lease an entire channel in your local market. Rates will vary depending on the size of the market and the reach of the channel. A word of caution from someone who has spent a career programming 24/7 channels: it takes a lot of content to have a full-time channel. And there is a lot involved in securing the rights to air shows. And the cost of production needs to be factored in on top of securing the channel. My advice is start with buying an hour on a local sub-channel and working your way up. I am a big believer in the crawl, walk, and then run approach to content marketing. Start with something small you can manage and work your way up.

Broadcast TV is not done reinventing itself. NextGen TV or ATSC 3.0 is currently being rolled out across the country. The major broadcasting companies have joined forces to create the Pearl TV Consortium to share technology and set the US standards for NextGen TV. Like the conversion to digital, NextGen TV will require a new receiver in the older TV sets. You can purchase an ATSC 3.0 tuner now. Newer Smart TVs already have an ATSC 3.0 tuner built in. South Korea rolled out the new form of broadcasting for the 2018 Winter Olympics and a lot of TVs are manufactured in that part of the world.

There is no mandatory transition date, so it is unclear how long before ATSC 3.0 will be the standard. But the new broadcasting will allow for 4K content and even more sub-channels. Imagine each broadcast station being able to offer up to thirty channels. The signal will also have a digital watermark, and an advanced emergency alert system that will wake up devices in geo-targeted areas to report emergencies.

There will also be opportunities for advertisers to target ads using the new technology.

Bottom line, don't write off broadcast TV as something from the past. Advertising on live, over-the-air TV is a great option for local businesses. Content marketing is also great if you have the budget to produce a local

TV show or go big and lease a digital sub-channel. As with all marketing options, ask questions about demographics and reach.

Cable TV's Future

CABLE TV IS defined as paid TV that is delivered via a local cable system, satellite, or digital fiber.

The first cable systems were designed to enhance the over-the-air signals of local TV stations. In areas like Arkansas, Oregon, and Pennsylvania in the late 1940s, community antennas were erected on high points and wires connected the homes to the antenna. So, if you lived in the valley and could not get the local TV stations, you could connect to a cable that ran to a high point where the large antenna would help you get television.

By the time the 1960s rolled around, there was a growing concern from local TV stations that cable systems would bring in competition from other markets. The FCC stepped in and placed restrictions on the industry.

According to the California Cable & Telecommunications Association, the FCC started to back off the restrictions with pressure from the federal, state, and local levels. The cable industry developed new satellite technology that made delivering content to local markets easier. In 1972 the nation's first pay-TV network was launched: Home Box Office, or HBO for short. HBO would later lead the move to direct-to-consumer paid TV in the new millennium.

Atlanta entrepreneur Ted Turner jumped at the new technology and took his local TV station, WTBS national. Airing the Atlanta Braves and classic movies, WTBS became the first "superstation." Turner would go on to launch the first 24/7 Cable News Network (CNN) in 1980.

But it wasn't until the 1984 Cable Act that the industry started to take hold of the content market share. Congress wanted to promote competition and deregulate the cable television industry. The Act gave power to the local cities on who would grant franchise licenses for cable operations. This meant the cable companies needed permission from each city they wanted to serve. It also ensured the local communities' needs and interests would be met.

If cable system X wanted to broadcast in your local community, they needed a franchise license from your city government.

The 1984 Cable Act led to what the CCTA describes as "the largest private construction project since World War II." More than $15 billion was spent on wiring American communities for cable. Billions more was spent on program development. Subscriber count went from sixteen million homes at the beginning of the decade to nearly fifty-three million by the end of the 1980s. And the number of channels increased from twenty-eight to seventy-nine during the same period.

It was during this time my family first got cable. I remember watching Nickelodeon, TBS, and MTV. MTV actually played music videos in the 1980s. And TBS ran syndicated shows like *Gilligan's Island*, and *The Brady Bunch*.

Cable TV continued to grow in the 1990s with 171 different channels and about seven in ten households subscribed. That was more than sixty-five million who were now paying for TV. My wife's family growing up was one of the three in ten families who did not have cable. My father-in-law was on staff at a local church and told his kids, "The day I have cable TV in my house is the day I have beer in the refrigerator and *Playboy* magazines on my coffee table." Years later, when we were married and came to visit my in-laws, we noticed they had satellite TV. My wife asked and my father-in-law replied with a smile, "It's not cable TV, it's satellite."

Satellite TV was originally used for commercial use, to deliver channels to the local cable systems for distribution to the consumer. But the DirecTVs and the Dish TVs you often think about when you hear the term "Satellite TV" were launched in 1994.

I was in college in the 1990s in a small Texas town that did not have any local TV channels and the local cable system had not been updated since it launched in the 1980s, so it had a very limited number of channels. Satellite TV was a great option for us to watch content.

Much has been written about the decline in the cable and satellite industry. Consumers want control of what channels they pay for; and more and more Americans are "cord cutters," a term used to describe people who drop cable.

According to a May 2021 Forbes article, "The number of homes that have traditional pay-TV has fallen to 75.6 million, down from 96.9 million just four years earlier." And that number is likely to continue to fall as consumers have more options today than ever before.

If you are considering marketing your business on cable, here are a few things to keep in mind. It is more cost effective to advertise on local cable than to advertise on a national cable channel. Each cable system has local avails they can sell you. In fact, the local avails are broken down by what the industry calls a "headend."

A cable television headend is where the cable company sources content for distribution to a local or regional neighborhood. Larger metropolitan areas have multiple headends. This allows the cable company to air different spots in each headend. So, if you own a local restaurant and you only want to advertise in your area, the local cable company can sell you spots only for your headend.

Buying local cable is also a more affordable option than airing your commercial spots on a popular cable channel. Rather than buying TBS or Fox News nationally, you can buy local cable spots.

As for content marketing, most local cable channels have channels you can purchase time on, but they don't typically draw a large viewership.

The Future of Paid TV

DON'T FEEL SORRY for the cable industry, they own the internet lines. We will talk about the world of Internet TV in Chapter Six.

I also don't believe cable or satellite TV is going away. While broadcasting is growing again, all the buildings in places like New York City make it hard to receive a clear antenna signal. Drive down a street in

Brooklyn and you will see satellite dishes on just about every brownstone. Some consumers like the ease of paying one bill to watch all the content they desire. As we will unpack in the world of Internet TV, you are not saving as much money as you once thought.

It will be interesting to watch what the major broadcasting networks do in the future. The FCC must-carry rule is an option. Under the must-carry rule the cable company does not pay for the content. ABC, NBC, CBS, and FOX have all waived their right to must-carry and charge fees instead. Remember the taxation model we discussed in Chapter One? If you subscribe to cable, part of your cable bill is going to channels you get for free over-the-air.

Will the major broadcast stations continue to offer their content for free over-the-air? Some have argued that networks will take their premium content online and charge a fee. I personally don't see this happening because the networks need good programming to attract viewers, which in turn attract advertisers.

Paid TV is moving online, and we will discuss the skinny bundles and internet options for cable in Chapter Six.

Conclusion

VIDEO IS A very powerful medium. America is a visual nation and advertising on local TV, local cable, or national TV on cable or satellite is still a good option.

Take the time to understand what demographic you are trying to reach and then ask a lot of questions to make sure the platform you are considering will deliver you the prospects you need to grow your business.

TV advertising can be expensive, but there are options available to still reach prospects at a budget you can afford. Consider digital sub-channels when buying on a budget. When purchasing commercials, be prepared to run your spot for at least thirteen weeks, three to four times a day. You need to be frequent and consistent when running ads on TV.

There is a formula to the perfect commercial, and we will discuss that in the next chapter.

Content marketing is a great option for growing a brand. Instead of advertising in someone else's TV show, create your own content and control the conversation. I have helped financial planners, real estate brokers, and several other small businesses launch a TV show that helps them connect with current customers and draw in prospective clients. I will have some tips for you to consider in Chapter Eleven.

5

ADVERTISING

ADVERTISING IS PROGRAMMING. When done right it leaves consumers with a positive impression of your product or service. Not all ads have to be humorous to be effective, but often it is the funny commercials that get etched into our memories.

When I think of great advertising campaigns, the first one that comes to mind is the Energizer Bunny. Introduced in 1989 as a parody of a Duracell commercial, the Energizer Bunny was named a Top Brand Icon by Advertising Age in 1999 and was inducted into the Madison Avenue Wall of Fame in 2017.

In my opinion, what made it so successful was how the Energizer Bunny was rolled out. I remember watching the then still new FOX Network when I first saw a commercial with the Bunny. For the next two or three "commercials" the Energizer Bunny would interrupt the spot with an announcer saying, "Nothing outlasts the Energizer, they keep going and going and going." As we will discuss in this chapter, it takes the average viewer several impressions before they recognize the brand in a commercial and process the call to action. The Energizer Bunny campaign was very successful with instant brand recognition.

You can't think about commercials without thinking about the Super Bowl. It's amazing to me that we have a major sporting event where more Americans are interested in the commercials than they are the game itself.

One of my all-time favorite Super Bowl ads was the 1993 McDonalds spot that featured Larry Bird challenging Michael Jordan to a basketball shooting contest for a Big Mac. Maybe it's because I am a Dallas Cowboy fan and our team beat the Buffalo Bills by thirty-five points, but that series of commercials was funny and stuck in my mind. Throughout the telecast you watched the two NBA legends compete for the hamburger.

And it's not just TV; radio has had its share of great commercials over the years. Amazon promoted its online bookstore with a series of creative radio spots to highlight the volume of books that Amazon had available online. The spots featured an actor calling different locations to see if they could find a place large enough to house the library.

Just like a good radio or TV program, a well produced commercial spot is nostalgic. Hear a jingle from an ad and you are transported back to your youth. "Plop Plop, Fizz Fizz, oh what a relief it is." "Snap, Crackle, Pop…. Rice Krispies." "I Wish I Was an Oscar Mayer Weiner."

History of Advertising

THE FIRST PAID radio advertisement in the United States cost Queensboro Corporation $50 to promote the sale of apartments in the Jackson Heights area. In 1922, $50 was good for fifty minutes on WEAF radio. The first paid ad to air in the United Kingdom wasn't until 1973. The BBC Radio was programmed as a public service; more than fifty years of commercial-free information and entertainment. Similar to the model you still see today on Public Broadcasting Service (PBS) or National Public Radio (NPR).

The first paid TV advertisement was for Bulova Watches on July 1, 1941. Nearly 4,000 baseball fans were tuned in to WNBT in New York to watch their Brooklyn Dodgers take on the Philadelphia Phillies. The spot reportedly cost between $4 and $9 to create and lasted only ten seconds.

Viewers saw a black and white image of the US with a clock over the plains states that had the Bulova logo on the clock. An announcer read the line, "America runs on Bulova time."

Dwight Eisenhower was the first to use TV to win the White House. Roy Disney turned his slogan "I like Ike" into a catchy song.

Other advertisers started using jingles in the 1960s to promote their brands. Mr. Potato Head was the first toy advertised on TV in 1952. RCA launched an ad for a color television set in 1965. In 1971, cigarette ads were banned on TV and Radio, but you will still find tobacco ads in print today.

Famous commercials include Coca-Cola's "Mean Joe Greene" spot that aired during the Super Bowl in 1979. Apple's Macintosh computers were introduced in a 1984 commercial during the big game and Steve Jobs sold $155 million new Macs in just three months. The same year, Wendy's rolled out their "Where's the Beef?" ad that was listed in my marketing textbook in college as the ultimate example of a great campaign. Wendy's was facing bankruptcy until the ad ran on TV and the company had a record $76.2 million in sales.

A 1968 ad for Tootsie Pop asked the question, "How many licks does it take to get to the center of a Tootsie Pop?" With each cartoon animal not being able to answer the boy's question, the owl at the end of the commercial volunteers to find out and bites into the Tootsie Pop after three licks. Then the announcer concludes that "the world may never know" the answer.

In 1956, the video cassette recorder (VCR) was invented. The ability for the consumer to record shows off live TV for playback later was not well received by Hollywood studios. In 1976, Universal City Studios and the Walt Disney Company sued Sony over the release of the Betamax VCR. Courts ruled against the studios, stating that non-commercial recording was legal. The studios won an appeal in 1981, and Sony took the case to the United States Supreme Court.

The Supreme Court Justices ruled in 1984 that home recording of television programs for later viewing constituted "fair use." Game on.

VCR sales took off and now viewers could record shows and watch them on their own time. That also meant that TV advertisements could be skipped.

Later the VCR was replaced with DVD players, which were not great at recording and playing back live TV. I remember my wife and I purchasing a DVD and VCR combo which allowed us to watch rented movies on DVD and still record our favorite TV shows on the VCR.

But in 1998, Jim Barton and Mike Ramsey invented the TiVo, the first digital video recorder, or DVR. Cable companies tried to stop the DVRs but gave in and released their own DVRs in set-top boxes. TiVo owned the patent and sued everyone. But more importantly the DVR made it even easier for the viewer to skip commercials.

Types of Commercials

MOST BUSINESS OWNERS understand what a radio or television commercial is, but they may not know there are three different types of commercials.

Brand advertisements are all about building brand recognition and customer loyalty over the lifetime of the consumer. When you see a commercial for companies like McDonald's, Coca-Cola, Ford, or State Farm, these are examples of brand commercials.

A lot of research and attention to details goes into a national brand campaign. The idea is to create a strong emotional connection with the product or services offered.

McDonald's ran an ad campaign with the slogan, "I'm loving it." The spots showed people smiling and enjoying McDonald's food. The brand association is connecting the emotion of happiness with going to their restaurants and enjoying their food.

Coca-Cola ran a campaign, "Share a Coke," connecting their brand with something you enjoy with a friend. From Coke's own website, "The purpose of the campaign was to create a more personal relationship with consumers and inspire shared moments of happiness."

Ford is "Built Ford Tough," to build a brand connection that the Ford line of trucks are built to last. And "Like a Good Neighbor, State Farm is There," is to build brand awareness that State Farm is owned by local agents who are there when you need them the most.

We all know the brands mentioned, so why do they still spend millions of dollars on advertising today? Do I need to be reminded of McDonald's or Coca-Cola? Keeping their brands front of mind is an important part of the brand campaigns. But building new loyal consumers is the main goal of all brand commercials.

The most targeted demographic for major brands is eighteen to twenty-four-year-olds. The logic behind this strategy is to start building brand loyalty when the consumer has their first paycheck and can start making buying decisions. As an example, Mom or Dad may have always bought Levi Jeans, because they have spent a lifetime being brand loyal to Levis. Their kids may want to try another brand of jeans once they have their own money. So, advertisers want to market to this age group.

That is not true of all brands. Certain products or services are not consumed or needed until later in life. AARP is not building brand loyalty with eighteen-year-olds. They do spend money targeting people as young as forty to start planting seeds for their services. I remember when my wife and I turned forty and started getting AARP ads in the mail. That was a wake up call in the Miller household. "Am I really old enough to get AARP advertisements?"

Local brand advertising is also more universal. If a local restaurant wants to reach a family, they are targeting the entire family. A local furniture store offering a sale is targeting a mom and dad or a grandmother and grandfather more than the kids or grandkids.

Basically, a brand advertisement is a radio or television commercial that is designed to make the public aware of their products and services so when the consumer is ready to make a purchase, their products or services are top of mind.

National brand advertising is purchased off of ratings of the demographic the company is targeting.

A Direct Response (DR) advertisement is a campaign that has a strong call to action designed to get the consumer to make a purchase today. These are the radio spots where you hear a phone number or website repeated several times. On TV you have an 800-number you can call today or a website with a promo code for you to log in today and make a purchase.

DR spots often have a strong hook as well. If you call in the next five minutes you will get two of the same products, just pay separate shipping and handling.

DR commercials are very product-centered, selling a specific product for the home. But DR spots can also sell a service like insurance or the tort commercials that sell class action lawsuits.

Agencies purchase Direct Response off data per radio or TV station or network. Meaning they know where consumers are watching and buying their products or services. That 800-number you see is specific to the TV channel you are watching. Same with the 800-number you hear on the radio. Sometimes the website is unique to the channel you are watching, or they have a promo code that helps them track the point of sale.

We sell a lot of Direct Response ads on our TV networks, and I use the sales to gauge our viewership. When the phone continues to ring, the advertiser continues to purchase the spots. When our DR sales are up, I know we have viewers watching and engaged in our programming. When the numbers start to slip, we look at ways to freshen up our programming.

National advertisers purchase year-round but reserve their biggest television budgets for the colder months. When it is cold outside, people are inside watching TV. When it is warm outside, they are taking vacations, enjoying the pool, and are not in front of their TVs. That is why your favorite shows now wait until October to launch a new season. The weather starts to turn cooler and families are settled into their new autumnal pattern.

The final category of commercial spots is my least favorite, the Per-Inquiry or PI spots. These look and feel like DR spots, but the advertiser only pays the TV station "per-inquiry," meaning they do not pay for the commercial spot up front, but send a check afterwards based on the response of the ads.

PIs are my least favorite on the business side because there is not a guarantee your spots will even air, and when they do air you won't get the frequency and consistency needed to have a successful campaign.

The general rule of thumb is brand advertisements pay more and therefore get placed first when TV stations are building their commercial logs for the day. DR advertising gets placed second and PI spots only get placed in unsold inventory.

There is a new category we have seen emerge in recent years, which is a hybrid of brand and DR advertising. The company is spending money on a brand campaign but still tracking results on a per-network basis, whereas traditional brand campaigns just track the overall campaign success, not on a station-by-station basis.

What type of commercial spot is best for your business? I would recommend most businesses to build brand awareness for their products or services. Direct Response ad campaigns are good if you have a specific product you want to move right away, but the key is to have a good fulfillment department. It's best if you work with a DR agency that can handle the call volume and fulfillment. They have the research behind their buys to make sure you are getting the most for your marketing dollars.

Does Advertising Still Work?

WHEN I WAS in college studying communications, I was given the assignment to try to go a full twenty-four hours without consuming any media. A difficult task for me, given that I worked my way through college with a job at the local radio station. But the point of the project was clear: we consume media all day long.

Tammy Greenberg, the Senior Vice President of Business Development for the Radio Advertising Bureau (RAB) says, "Of people that have driven or ridden in a car in the past month, 75% listened to

AM/FM in the car, which is compared to Sirius XM 21%, podcasts 30%, online radio 33%, CD player 35%, and their owned digital music 48%. This is according to the 2021 Infinite Dial Report."

Overall radio media buys did decline in 2020 due to the pandemic. More people sheltering in place at home equaled less people commuting to work and listening to radio. Even still, the US and Canada sold $14.8 billion in radio advertising. A number expected to climb to $18.3 billion by 2023 according to PricewaterhouseCooper's annual Global Entertainment and Media Outlook.

Statista surveyed 3,000 respondents in March of 2021 ages eighteen and older and found 26 percent watched twelve hours or more of live TV. Nineteen percent watched three to five hours of live TV and only 14 percent said they did not watch any live TV. Nielsen estimates there are 121 million TV homes in the United States. That's homes, not total number of viewers. But combining that data shows an estimated 31.5 million homes have the TV on for live viewing for twelve hours or more a week.

TV advertising on linear television accounts for approximately 25 percent of the total US media ad revenue, accounting for $60 billion in ad sales in 2020. Overall media sales dipped by 15 percent in 2020 because of the pandemic, so those numbers are expected to climb as well.

Why would major brands spend billions of dollars on radio and television advertising if it was not working? I have spent my career on the network radio and TV side of the business, and I can assure you advertisers do not spend money for charity. If the campaign is not working, budgets get pulled.

Radio and Television advertising still work in the on-demand world we live in today. The key is good creativity. Remember, advertising is programming. I have been on my couch watching a show with my kids, when they ask me to stop fast-forwarding so they can watch their favorite commercial. Let that sink in for a moment.

TV networks and cable channels have also gotten smart on ways to get you to watch the commercial. NBC started making their first commercial break in each prime-time show only one minute with an announcement, "We will be back after this short one-minute break." Even before the NBC experiment, channels started to study viewing habits to see how long you need to watch a show before you are locked in for the half-hour or full hour. If you are into the show, you are less likely to change the channel and more likely to watch the commercial breaks. Then there is what I like to call "the DVR stoppers;" when the network runs a promo in the middle of the commercial break and I stop fast-forwarding thinking the break is over. I end up seeing one or two commercials before the program resumes.

When it comes to local radio or digital broadcast TV, there is no fast-forwarding during commercials. That is why I believe advertising local and on digital stations are a great option for business owners.

Finally, in an interesting way the Internet has retrained the consumers to expect commercials. Watch any video on YouTube and you have to either watch an entire fifteen-second commercial or you can skip a thirty-second commercial after five seconds.

The Perfect Spot

THE FIRST KEY to any successful advertising campaign is frequency and consistency. You have to run your commercial spots often and on a consistent basis to build brand loyalty.

The average consumer needs to hear or see your advertising spot seven times before they will fully understand the message and respond accordingly. I have read some studies that pushed that number as high as fourteen today, with so many advertising messages coming from a variety of sources.

The point is, airing one spot or a handful of spots is not a good use of your marketing dollars. And the length of your campaign needs to be at least thirteen weeks. Let's break it down this way: if a TV commercial aired three times a day for thirteen weeks, how often are you likely to see that commercial spot? You are not watching the same network all day long, so you might see the commercial Monday night and not see it again until Thursday night. If you need to see the ad at least seven times, how long before you notice the ad and respond?

That is why it is not enough to have your ad running frequently, you also have to run it consistently. You are trying to build brand loyalty for your business. That is not something that is done in a short window.

The biggest reason that radio or television advertising fails is the impatience of the business owner. They want instant success when any marketing effort is not instant. That is just a fact and if anyone tries to sell you a quick ROI on marketing, buyer beware. There are a lot of people that will promise you the world to take your money and never plan on delivering you results.

Erica Farber is the President and CEO of RAB. She told me of a story she shared with a prospect early in her radio career. The prospect told her that radio doesn't work, so they will never spend marketing dollars on radio. Farber smiled and jokingly said, "Then you will be okay if we run an ad on the station telling listeners to not visit your restaurant because of health concerns." The prospect was quick to say, "You can't do that!" Of course, Erica would never run such an ad, but she made her point.

Again, the reason why most campaigns don't work has nothing to do with the outlet. Radio and TV stations can show you the demographics of who is watching or listening, but you have to be patient in giving the campaign time to start to yield results.

Once a campaign starts to get leads for the business, it is a steady source of new leads every month. That is why you see the same local businesses advertise every month. They were patient and used the radio or TV station to build brand loyalty and they continue to build brand loyalty by running more ads.

The second key to a successful campaign is matching your product with the right programming. Seems simple enough but do your market research. A good media salesperson will make sure they are placing your ads in the right shows, but it is good for you to know what questions to ask and do a little homework yourself. If the media salesperson is only interested in their commission, they will sell you any spot you are willing to purchase.

For example, if you own a local coffee shop and your research shows your number-one demographic is women ages thirty-five to fifty-five, you would not want to advertise in a hunting show that is geared toward men ages twenty-five to forty-five.

I had a well-intentioned salesperson try to sell an eyelash extension business a commercial package in one of our local markets. BizTV is 64 percent male, with 43 percent of our viewers between the ages twenty-five and forty-four and 33 percent aged forty-five to sixty-four. They are interested in employment issues, advertising services, and financial investments. Not exactly the perfect demographic for eyelash extensions. I would not let her take the business. We were not the right fit for that prospect.

There are several options out there for you, just make sure the programming is drawing in the type of prospect you are trying to reach.

The final key to having the perfect spot is writing the perfect script. There are four basic components to every commercial script.

The Hook

The Need or Problem

The Solution

The Call to Action

The hook is what gets the attention of the listener or viewer. How is your commercial spot going to stand out amongst the other spots? Hooks can be eye catching, use humor, be silly or sometimes shocking depending on the product. Sometimes the hook is just storytelling.

An eye-catching hook can use colors to get viewers' attention, a technique often used by Apple. You might see several iPhones rolling around in a circle with bright colors. Or an eye-catching hook could show you a majestic scene. I think about a commercial that showed the Anheuser-Busch Clydesdale horses galloping on a snow-covered field as the spot opened.

Humor is a popular hook but writing for comedy is challenging and if not written or performed well, what seemed funny to your staff can come across as corny to the viewers. So, if you are going to take this approach, hire a professional production crew to write and shoot your commercial.

Some examples of humor include just about every insurance commercial on television today. State Farm starts their commercials off with local residents giving their State Farm agent extra benefits to show their appreciation for the low insurance rates. Progressive will have a humorous shot of Flo and her team on the beach. Farmers will show you a crazy accident they have covered before. Allstate will show you mayhem. Insurance companies have large advertising budgets.

Silly hooks may make you laugh, but often leave you scratching your head. Mountain Dew had a Super Bowl ad they ran in 2016 that opened with a creature that was a cross between a puppy, a monkey, and a baby. The tagline was, "Three Awesome Things Combined" to promote the new Mountain Dew Kickstart Midnight Grape drink. I am still having nightmares about that thing licking one of the actors as he chanted, "Puppy, Monkey, Baby."

A shocking ad might be used to promote an advocacy group. I think about the spots that show the animals who have been abused to raise awareness of animal cruelty.

Storytelling hooks open with a story that draws in the viewer. In the 1984 Presidential election, Ronald Reagan's campaign ran a spot called, "It's Morning Again in America." The hook showed a peaceful boat on a lake with a city landscape in the background and a voice that read, "It's morning again in America."

Hooks are an important part to getting the attention of the listener or viewer.

Next, you want to present a need or a problem that needs solving. What does your product or service fulfill? That is the need or problem your spot should address.

If you own a restaurant, the need might be family time to sit and enjoy a meal without distractions. If you own a car repair garage, the need might be making sure the teenage driver's car is safe to be on the road.

If you are a doctor, the problem could be showing the stats of residents who die from a preventable heart attack.

In any good sales process, present the need or problem before you present a solution. That is sales 101 and a commercial advertisement is sales!

Once a need or problem has been identified, next you present your solution. What makes your company unique in solving that need? How are you different from your competition that is working to meet the same need?

If you only have thirty seconds, choose your words carefully and focus on what makes you worth earning the viewers trust and business. I personally would not focus on phrases like, "locally owned since 1929." If you have built a brand that is known for being involved in the community, then reminding viewers you have been around for a while might be a good option to set you apart from your competition. But if your competition has been around longer or that does not fit your brand, use the time you have to better sell on what makes your business special.

The final element is the most important: the call to action. This is where you give listeners or viewers the clear path you want them to take to do business with you.

If there is no clear call to action, how can you measure the success of the commercial?

A call to action example is, "Call today for your free, no obligation estimate." Or Geico Insurance who has a great call to action: "Fifteen minutes could save you 15% or more on car insurance." The call to action is to call and save money.

In the Dallas-Fort Worth area we have a local car dealer named Clay Cooley. His call to action is, "Shop me last, shop me first, either way come see Clay." The call to action is to come see Clay to get a quote on a new or used car.

You can also use call to actions to offer something unique to that campaign to track results. "Go online and mention this ad to receive

5 percent off your purchase." Or, "stop by and tell them I sent you for a free soft drink or tea with your meal."

These are just some examples to get you thinking about your perfect commercial spot.

Conclusion

RADIO AND TELEVISION commercials have been around for decades, and they are still effective today. Even in the world of DVRs and on-demand content, people still listen to live radio and watch live TV.

There are different types of commercial spots depending on your needs. Brand awareness campaigns are the most common for local businesses, but direct response advertising works when you are selling a specific product or service that can be fulfilled online or shipped directly to the consumer.

Be patient if you are going to run radio or TV spots. To be effective you have to run the spots frequently and consistently. It takes time to build brand awareness, but once you do you can expect a steady flow of new sales for your business.

Make sure you do your research and run your commercials in programs that match the demographics you are trying to reach.

Finally, every commercial spot needs a good hook, present a need or problem, a solution that shows why your business is the best choice, and a clear call to action.

When you go to buy time on radio or TV, refer back to earlier chapters on ratings so you understand what you are buying.

6

THE NEW OTT WORLD

MY WIFE AND I have always enjoyed watching movies together. When we were first married we would go to the local video rental store to select a couple of films for the weekend. But around the time our oldest was born I heard about this new service, Netflix, that would mail us movies. We logged on and selected all the movies we wanted to see and put them into a priority list. We paid for the option to have one movie delivered at a time instead of the more expensive plan of multiple DVDs at a time; after all we had a newborn and most of our money went to diapers.

But the experience was frustrating. Movies would often get delayed because we had either maxed out on our number of movies that month or the next-in-line DVD was not available. Blockbuster was around the corner, and they entered the DVD membership model by offering the same plan, but with a twist. We could return the movies to the brick-and-mortar Blockbuster and get the next DVD mailed out to us faster.

In the meantime, Netflix was working on a new model that launched in 2007: taking their entire library of movies online. Now we could stream as many movies as we wanted, but you had to watch them on a computer. At least that is what we thought was the only option.

The first time we had a Netflix app available on our TV was when we purchased a new BluRay player that came with some built-in apps. Now our weekends were spent looking for something we wanted to watch, and not actually watching anything. All kidding aside, our entire family loved the new streaming option. And soon we discovered other apps like Vudu, which allowed us to rent new movies and purchase digital copies of movies that we can watch anytime.

Netflix led the charge to move content from traditional delivery methods like cable, satellite, or broadcast, to the internet. And the term OTT was born.

What is OTT?

THE TERM OTT stands for Over the Top, an industry vernacular used to describe content that is delivered via the internet. Why not call it Internet TV? I am sure some engineer coined this phrase, but it simply means to deliver content over the top of the existing internet. It also refers to the fact that the content is being delivered over the top of someone else's platform. Whereas cable delivers content on lines they control, Netflix delivers content over the internet, which is not owned by Netflix. Thus, Netflix is delivering content to you over the top of someone else's platform. OTT.

OTT is an umbrella term that covers a lot of subcategories to include streaming boxes, SVOD, AVOD, Virtual MVPDs, and FAST channels.

Let's unpack this new and growing world of OTT platforms. Once you understand how the market is shifting, you can start to think of ways you can market your business using OTT channels.

Streaming Devices

ROKU WAS FOUNDED in 2002 as an LLC by Anthony Wood. Mr. Wood still worked for Netflix when he founded Roku but left the company in

2008 and launched the first streaming player when his former company decided not to get into the hardware space.

Roku offered consumers a new alternative to traditional cable, as the Roku device could be hooked directly to your TV and connect to the internet either directly or via Wi-Fi. It came preloaded with apps like Netflix, and to this day Roku has an open-source business model, meaning anyone can create an app and distribute content out via Roku.

As of the second quarter of 2021, Roku reported fifty-five million active users in the United States alone. As of the writing of this book, there are more than 26,000 apps available for download on Roku. That number is only climbing.

Apple launched Apple TV in 2007. The first Apple box came with a 40 GB hard disk for storing movies. Future generations would be rolled out in 2010 and 2012. Apple's product allows iPhone users to connect the device to their iCloud account and easily control TV with their smartphone and/or Apple Watch and cast content from their device to their TV. The term "cast" is used when you play content on your phone, but instead of seeing it on your phone you watch it on your TV. Thus, you are "casting" the image onto your TV.

As a side note, Apple released Macintosh TV in 1993. Not a streaming platform, but Apple worked with Sony to have a computer monitor with a built-in Sony TV that users could switch over to and watch cable TV. Steve Jobs was a visionary!

Google TV was released in 2010 and has gone through multiple iterations. It is now called Android TV, which was launched in 2014. Google integrated smartphones into their platforms with the product Chromecast. Users run content off their phones and cast them onto their TVs.

Amazon introduced Fire TV in 2014, now known as Amazon Fire TV.

Those are the major streaming OTT boxes on the market today: Roku, Apple TV, Google, and Amazon. You can debate which ones are best for you as a consumer, but they all have their benefits. Working in the industry, I try to keep up with all the trends. I own a couple of Roku devices, an Apple TV, and an Amazon Fire TV.

Roku is the cheapest on the market. You can purchase a Roku device for as low as $25, though they have also released more expensive models. We recently purchased the Roku sound bar, which improves the audio quality and streams content in 4k.

Amazon Fire retails a little higher than Roku devices but works with your Amazon Alexa devices. That is a cool feature in our home, because it pauses live TV any time there is an announcement over the Alexa devices. We have our Amazon Fire Stick in the TV room where our daughters watch TV, so when we "announce" dinner is ready, the Fire Stick will pause their show with the audio announcement as well as written out across the screen. Parent bonus.

You can also pull up content via your Alexa devices and the Amazon Fire TV has a better voice command remote.

Apple TV is my personal favorite, but I also own an iPhone, Apple Watch, and Mac Air. Yes, I am one of those Apple nerds. Thus, I do not have a Google or Android TV in my house.

But really the device is just a preference; at the end of the day they all deliver the same content to your TV. You can get Netflix, Disney+, Hulu, and all the other popular OTT channels or apps on all the above devices.

Your smartphone is also an OTT streaming device. You can download all your favorite apps and watch content from anywhere. If you are like me and love content, this is an amazing time to be alive. Don't be surprised to catch me checking in on a broadcast of a college football game while I am sitting in the stands watching another game live. Yes, I am that guy.

There are new emerging platforms on the way. The broadcast and cable platforms are rolling out their own streaming boxes as well, so if you subscribe to cable today you might get a streaming box instead of the traditional cable box. This gives subscribers the option to watch traditional cable and switch over to streaming channels like Netflix without having to switch devices.

From a marketing standpoint, there are some options for you. You can purchase ads that run on platforms like Roku. You can create screens that users can upload with your logo. My family likes to take cruises and we found a home screen from our favorite cruise line on Roku. I loaded it to our Rokus ahead of a family vacation one year. You can work with Roku directly, but I recommend you work with an agency that knows how to navigate the buy and can help you design the creative.

SVODs

An svod is a Subscriber Video on Demand service, where members pay a monthly fee to watch unlimited amounts of content commercial free. Again, Netflix is the OG of SVODs, where more than 209 million subscribers pay a monthly fee globally, as of Q2 2021. In the United States and Canada alone, there are seventy-four million subscribers.

Amazon not only has their own streaming device in the Amazon Fire TV, but they also offer their own streaming channel or app. Amazon Prime TV comes with Amazon Prime membership, and there are 200 million subscribers worldwide as of Q2 2021, with 126 million in the United States alone.

Disney+ is still new to the space, but already boasts 116 million subscribers as of Q3 2021. Peacock Premium is also a new player but has used the power of NBC's broadcast and cable channels to welcome fifty-four million US subscribers, as of Q2 of 2021.

HBO and HBO Max, one of the original paid TV channels on cable, was the first to go direct-to-consumer with their content, meaning you no longer had to pay for HBO through a cable provider. They now have forty-seven million subscribers in the United States, as of Q2 2021.

Prior to HBO's move into direct-to-consumer streaming, none of the cable channels dared to venture into this space. The reason was simple: their agreements with the cable companies prohibited that option. Working in the industry I can tell you that cable companies fought this move to the internet, threatening to drop any channel that violated the clause. The cable industry's answer to the internet was "TV Everywhere," where cable customers could watch their favorite channels over streaming devices or their smartphones, only if they logged in through their cable provider. Still today, there are several popular cable channels that you can watch directly, only if you log in through your cable provider.

When HBO went direct, we all watched to see what the major cable companies would do in response. They did nothing. Why? The big cable companies realized they owned the internet lines, so in a sense they were still making money off HBO. Remember when your internet bill was $20 a month and your cable bill was $100 a month? Now look at your internet bill. And most cable companies will offer you video as an add-on for less than they used to charge.

Centerpost Media owns a couple of independent TV channels. When you are independent it is hard to get coverage against the major media groups who continue to add more channels. I lobbied in Washington and met with the FCC on record about this topic in 2014, when a couple of major cable mergers were taking place. We took the stance for the cable companies because we felt they were being forced to add more channels under threat of losing channels from the major media companies. We got a lot of sympathy from some politicians on the hill, and we were told we might have a case. But going to court is an expensive endgame.

As more and more content has moved to the internet, the major cable companies are less interested in adding more channels. Today independent channels are told they already have coverage via the internet, something that used to bother me, but the truth is they are right. More and more consumers watch content directly from the source versus an additional paid cable service. That is why we launched our own SVOD channels in 2015.

Hulu+ is another popular SVOD service, with forty-two million US subscribers. Apple TV+ does not report subscriber numbers, but the estimates are around forty million subscribers. Like Amazon, Apple has both a streaming device and a streaming channel or app. Apple TV is the device you purchase to watch content and Apple TV+ is the streaming channel.

SVOD channels are great if you want to watch content without commercials, but not so great if you want to advertise your business. There are no commercials. But if you want to use content to drive business, don't rule out an SVOD channel. I am seeing more small businesses launch a Roku channel that is available for free or a small subscriber fee. They are creating content and using social media to drive viewership. The content is centered around their business concept. A bit outside of the box for most small businesses, but an option to keep an eye on as you create more content.

AVODs

LIKE SVOD, IN that they offer only videos on demand, AVODs are Advertising-Based Video on Demand platforms. The content is offered for free but is supported through commercial advertising.

Popular AVODs include Sony Crackle, tubi TV, Vudu, and The CW.

Hulu offers a hybrid service. You can pay Hulu a smaller monthly fee and watch videos on demand with commercials. Hulu+ is the premium service that is commercial free.

In 2019, advertisers spent $7.9 billion in the US alone on AVODs. One of the largest growing advertising platforms, some estimates say the annual amount is expected to exceed $24.2 billion by 2025.

This is where the programmatic advertising comes into play, which we will unpack later in this chapter. But if you are a local business there are options for you to advertise in this space. Hulu has rolled out a direct-to-consumer product in 2021, where local businesses can advertise on Hulu. I believe this will become more and more of an option for advertisers looking to run television commercials in their market.

Virtual MVPDs

AN MVPD IS an industry term that means Multichannel Video Programming Distributor, or what you might think of as a cable or satellite system. So, a virtual MVPD is basically a cable system where the content is delivered via the internet versus the traditional cable or satellite.

Where VODs only deliver video content on demand, the MVPDs offer a package of streaming channels as well as some VOD content. Again, they act just like your traditional cable system.

DISH Network launched the first Virtual MVPD in 2015: Sling TV. Sling has about 2.47 million subscribers in the United States as of Q1 2021, but it's not the largest Virtual MVPD.

Hulu+ Live TV has four million subscribers as of Q1 2021, followed by YouTube TV with three million US subscribers, Philo with 800 thousand, AT&T Now (formally DirecTV Now) with 656 thousand, and Fubo TV with 547 thousand subscribers.

These numbers have not passed those of traditional cable subscribers. As of Q3 2021, DISH has 8.55 million subscribers, DirecTV has 15.4 million, Comcast has 18.96 million, and Spectrum has 15.42 million subscribers. While the number of people leaving cable is growing, cable subscriber numbers are still much larger than the Virtual MVPD numbers, but smaller than the SVOD and AVOD numbers, which can be misleading.

When I attended the PAID TV show in Denver in 2019, trade show experts reported that on average, a home will subscribe to two major SVODs and one or two smaller SVODs. Meaning these subscriber counts are overlapping. A cable subscriber is likely to also subscribe to Netflix, Hulu, Disney+, or all of the above.

There are two major driving factors leading to "cord cutters." The first is the rising cost of video content. When cable companies were in a race to provide as much content as possible, they added more and more channels. Each channel has a per-subscriber fee the cable company has to pay each month. Refer to the taxation model we discussed in Chapter One. Add more channels, add more expenses. And the cable companies passed those expenses on to the cable customer, raising the cost of the monthly cable bill. The existing channels also raised their monthly rate with each contract negotiation to cover the rising cost of paying for actors and production. Again, the cable company passed the extra cost on to the cable subscriber.

The second reason for cutting the cord is wanting more control over what channels are available to the consumer. Like the first reason, the cable customer started to question why they were paying for content they never watched.

That is when the "skinny bundle" was introduced through the Virtual MVPDs. The "skinny bundle" offered consumers fewer channels at a lower rate. You could pay DISH a smaller monthly fee and subscribe to Sling TV. Fewer channels, but it included a nice selection of the most popular cable channels.

My family cut the cord in spring of 2018. We had been a long-time DirecTV subscriber, but realized our kids mainly watched Netflix. Why were we paying more than $120 a month for TV, when we mainly watched content that was offered for free over-the-air? As a sports fan, I still wanted to make sure I got ESPN and Fox Sports. We subscribed to PlayStation Vue and paid about $50 a month. The kids didn't miss DirecTV. My wife still got the channels she wanted, and I never missed a game. Unfortunately, Sony was losing money and pulled the plug on PlayStation Vue. Remember, sports are expensive, so at $50 a month Sony lost more money with each new subscriber. Their plan was to slowly raise the monthly price.

And therein lies the problem with Virtual MVPDs. The cost per subscriber for channels is the same for the cable companies, whether it's on traditional cable or a virtual cable system. We now subscribe to YouTube TV, and we have watched our monthly bill creep up to $65 a month. Still cheaper than traditional cable, but I wonder how long before our monthly bill is back to more than $100 a month.

The truth is we are close now. FOMO, or the fear of missing out, is causing a lot of consumers like us to subscribe to multiple SVODs in addition to our Virtual MVPD. One person at that trade show put it perfectly, "The plus in the name means you need that service plus something else." We have YouTube TV, Disney+, Hulu+, and ESPN+. We also subscribe to Netflix and Apple TV+ on and off through the year, and we are Amazon Prime members, so we get Prime TV. Are we really saving money?

I would not be in the least bit surprised to see a shift back to paying a single provider for content, but I don't see us going back to traditional cable or satellite. As a business owner you need to follow the trends. Where are your prospects going so you know where to spend your marketing dollars?

Virtual MVPDs are a great option to advertise your business. Like AVODs, you can purchase programmatic ads if you are a large company. And there will be more and more options for smaller companies to start to advertise their business in this space. The good news is that when it's digital you have the most accurate data. Everything online is trackable, so services like Sling TV and YouTube TV can tell you exactly how many people are watching a particular channel or program.

FAST Channels

FAST CHANNELS STANDS for Free Ad Supported Television. Similar to AVOD, but AVODs are ad-supported video-on-demand channels where FAST Channels are streams.

Tom Ashley is the CEO of Invincible Entertainment Partners. His company helps businesses create FAST Channels and they will distribute the channels through his platform Galaxy. Ashley says FAST Channels are like Virtual MVPDs, but there is a difference. "FAST is pretty much structured and built programs all on an IP based system and delivered over the internet from a CDN and a server; everything happens online. Whereas broadcast would be delivered through a headend, sent to a satellite, and pulled down at various endpoints. So that would not be considered FAST, it would just be a traditional broadcast channel that's being delivered on a FAST service," he explained.

The other clear difference is FAST channels are free for the consumer, but Virtual MVPDs are not. Remember, services like Sling TV and YouTube TV must pay a per-subscriber fee for most of the channels they offer, so that is why they charge a subscriber fee. The Virtual MVPDs are making money from advertising. Most of the subscriber fees pay for the content.

There is a growing trend in the FAST Channel space. Pluto TV reports more than fifty-two million active monthly users, with advertising revenue hitting $502 million in Q2 of 2021. Pluto was launched as an independent service in 2013 but was purchased by Viacom for $340 million in January of 2019.

Other popular FAST channels include Xumo (owned by NBC), Peacock (owned by NBCU), The Roku Channel (owned by Roku) and Samsung TV+ (owned by Samsung).

Samsung TV+ is a huge player in the FAST channel space. New smart Samsung TVs come preloaded with FAST channels that viewers can watch along with antenna TV. It's like having a free cable TV service.

You will not find your large top twenty cable networks on FAST channels, or will you? Look at Pluto TV and you will recognize several cable channels that are now offered as a FAST channel. Viacom merged with CBS in December of 2019, almost a year after Viacom purchased Pluto. Now you can watch TV Land, MTV, Comedy Central, and CMT. To be clear, the Pluto channels run a different line-up from their cable channel cousins and have a slightly different name. MTV is MTV Pluto. But the content is similar. And because CBS owns Pluto, you can watch channels like the Star Trek Channel, the CSI Channel, and The Carol Burnett Show Channel.

Pluto plays ads based on the traffic that is watching the streams and the time of day. And believe me, they play a lot of commercials. For some it is too much, but for the consumer who wants to watch free TV and doesn't mind the ads, services like Pluto are a great option.

Are FAST channels good for the business owner? Anything that gives you the option to advertise your business is a good option. But understanding programmatic advertising is key.

Programmatic Advertising

WE BRIEFLY TOUCHED on this topic when looking at options for audio advertising, but programmatic ads are a growing trend as the consumer shifts to digital outlets.

In traditional broadcasting, commercials are sold weeks and sometimes days in advance. A salesperson would fill out an order form and pass it along to the traffic department. The traffic department is responsible for making sure each order gets filled during a broadcast day. If you recall, traffic departments place brand ads first, followed by direct response ads, and then per-inquiry commercials.

Once a traffic log is closed, it is sent to the network operations center for playout. When you watch a traditional TV channel or listen to a traditional radio station, you are either watching or listening to a program log played out on a computer. But once that log is finalized, there is no changing the commercial spot.

On our channels, we close the logs two days in advance of airtime. So, our traffic department is working on Wednesday's log on Monday. Sometimes they will temporarily hold a log if they know a last-minute order is coming in. During the holiday season we are on accelerated logs, meaning we close the logs days in advance to give our staff time away from the office.

That is not how programmatic ads work. With programmatic ads, the traffic department schedules what is known as SCTE-35 markers. The SCTE-35 markers indicate when to play commercial spots downstream. That means the traffic logs are closed without commercial spots on FAST channels.

Let me just unpack how crazy this concept is to traditional traffic departments. In 2011, I worked for a company that partnered with Mark Burnett to integrate social videos into a linear channel. My role was securing content for the new concept and managing the new programs and traffic schedules to include the social videos. Because our technology allowed viewers to record social videos with a few minutes of airtime, we needed the traffic department to close the logs without the commercial spots in-house. In essence we were asking an experienced broadcast traffic department to break one of the major rules in broadcasting: scheduling dead air.

On the back end the dead air was filled with social videos. You can imagine the conversation I had when I tried to explain to our traffic team that it would be okay to send the logs without the commercials.

Today, traditional networks like the ones we own run a hybrid traffic schedule. Our traffic team still schedules commercial spots for the linear feed to cable and broadcast affiliates, but they also place a SCTE-35 marker for our FAST channels to run programmatic ads.

Programmatic ads are all filled within seconds of airtime. Tom Ashley says it's an online auction that is taking place all day, driven by artificial intelligence. "It knows that these ad markers are coming up, and it will make a call to an ad server that it is about to have an ad break. Say it's a ninety-second ad break, that can be filled with three thirty-seconds or a thirty and a sixty-second spot. In a fraction of a second the server knows how many spots to fill and how many people are watching the channel right now. And then ad agencies, through a handful of companies, will bid on the airtime."

The highest bid will get placed first. Ad agencies determine ahead of time what their clients are willing to spend per CPM and what demographics their clients are trying to reach. The bidding process is done based on the information from the FAST channel's server and data passed along by the agencies.

The technology allows FAST channels to deliver more relative commercial ads. In the radio broadcasting world this is called copy splitting.

As an example, a Home Depot commercial run in December would look different depending on where you live. In the South, the spot might be promoting an outdoor fire pit. Up north, the Home Depot commercial might be pushing a snow blower. Agencies can also tag spots with local information, giving specific details on where a local store is located.

Programmatic also opens the door for retargeting ads, something we will discuss more in Chapter Nine when we look at digital marketing. But retargeting ads track the pattern of the consumer to send ads that are specific to what that consumer is looking to purchase. For example, when our family added a teenage driver to our insurance policy, we were shocked at what our current provider was going to charge us monthly. My wife and I started researching other insurance providers. Using our IP address, retargeted programmatic ads started popping up on YouTube TV for insurance companies, way more than usual. Every commercial break featured one or two insurance companies. Once we picked a policy, those ads were not as frequent. Some might find that creepy, but from the business owner's standpoint, it is marketing dollars well spent, targeting prospects who are looking to make a purchase soon.

The programmatic ads open the door for more localization, but currently there are not a lot of options for smaller businesses. It's more of a volume play and most local businesses don't have a large enough budget to play in this space. That is starting to change; as I mentioned you can now purchase ads directly with Hulu. But all other programmatic ads are placed by a handful of companies that advertising agencies work with to get their clients placed.

The other negative to placing programmatic ads is a lack of control as to when and how frequently your commercial spots air. Remember it is a bidding process, so if other advertisers are willing to pay more your spot does not air.

The good news is, you can go directly with any of the FAST channels and pay a higher rate but get guaranteed coverage. Like brand spots, direct spots will get placed ahead of programmatic spots.

Conclusion

THE TWO BIGGEST areas of growth in the video space are broadcast TV channels and OTT channels. There is still a large number of viewers who are paying for traditional cable and satellite TV, but more and more consumers are cutting the cord and watching free over-the-air TV and OTT channels.

The OTT numbers overlap, so even paying TV customers are subscribing to SVODs and tuning in to AVODs and FAST Channels.

As a business owner, understanding how these new mediums work will make you a smarter marketer of your brand. But like with all marketing options, the first thing you need to do is understand your target demographic. Who are you trying to reach? Study your current base of customers or survey them to get a better understanding of your ideal prospect.

Once you know who you are trying to reach, if you want to advertise in the OTT space, do your homework. Ask the content providers for details on their demographics and see if it's a match.

You can advertise directly on some of the streaming devices. You can reach out to any AVOD, Virtual MVPD, or FAST Channel and place your spots directly. You can also work with an ad agency to get your spots into the programmatic bidding process. Any national campaign will cost you more money, but some of these platforms can geofence your media buy to only cover the market you are trying to reach. It never hurts to ask!

On the content marketing side, pushing out your content to Roku is the easiest to set up if you have enough content for your own channel. If not, I recommend you reach out to other OTT channels about placing your content. We own Bizvod, one of the largest collections of small business and entrepreneur content. We sell time on Bizvod for businesses to push out content. And because Bizvod is available on all the major streaming devices (Roku, Apple TV, Android TV, Amazon Fire, iOS and Android Phones) it allows businesses to push current customers and prospects to their content.

7

THE WORLD WIDE WEB

WE TAKE FOR granted that most of the devices we own are connected to the internet. Beyond just our smartphones and laptops, our TVs, microwaves, and washing machines are all online today.

Seriously, our appliances are now online. We have yet to join the growing club of homes with a smart refrigerator, only because our current one still works. But when we needed to replace our microwave, I laughed when it came with an app and instructions to connect it online. Curious, I followed the instructions and now I can turn my microwave surface light on remotely. I have yet to use this beyond the first day I connected the appliance to my Wi-Fi. Same is true when we finally needed to replace our washing machine. There is an app we can download to let us know when the laundry has finished washing. We have never downloaded that app. Call us old school but we are still able to hear the tune it plays when the cycle is complete.

My girls have grown up in this connected world. When my oldest daughter was in elementary school, she asked me one day in amazement, "Dad, did you not have the internet when you were a kid?" I still laugh at that question.

The truth is we did have access to the internet when I was a kid, but it was nothing like you see today. We were connected to the internet in our schools, but the World Wide Web did not become a part of our daily lives until I was in college in the mid-1990s. And since then, we have seen the internet bubble come and go and watched how being connected has disrupted every area of our lives, including how we market our businesses.

History of the Internet

LIKE ALL TECHNOLOGY, the origins of the internet go further back in time than most of us realize, and not one person can claim to be the inventor of the internet.

The concept of a "world wireless system" was first mentioned in the early 1900s, long before the technology existed. Nikola Tesla is credited for being the first to discuss the idea.

Technology needs funding, and throughout history some of the best inventions were born out of a need for national security. In the 1950s, the United States was in the middle of a Cold War with the Soviet Union. As both superpowers built up their nuclear weapons, the US was searching for a way to send sensitive information that could not be intercepted by the Russians. Computers at the time were large, like the size of homes large, and mainly used by the military and universities. That meant the military had to travel to the computer to use it as a resource.

The resolution was the invention of time-sharing. Users could access a computer's mainframe through a series of terminals. It worked but was very limited. The U.S. Department of Defense formed ARPANET, or the Advanced Research Projects Agency Network. Using technology that had been developed by computer scientists in the 1960s known as "packet switching," the military could start to send information from one location to another in "packets," meaning the message would be divided up and reassembled on the receiving end.

The first message that ARPANET delivered was on October 29, 1969, from a computer located in the research lab of UCLA to a second computer located on the campus of Stanford. The message was one word, "LOGIN." The L and O were received and then the system crashed.

Internet technology improved in the 1970s when Robert Kahn and Vinton Cerf developed the Transmission Control Protocol and Internet Protocol, TCP/IP for short. These set the standards for how data would be communicated and were adopted by ARPANET on January 1, 1983. Researchers started to assemble networks based on the TCP/IP standards.

But it was Tim Berners-Lee that invented the World Wide Web. Not to be confused with the internet, the World Wide Web is the most common way you access data online in the form of websites and hyperlinks. When Mr. Berners-Lee introduced the new access point in 1990, it took the internet mainstream from military and university users to the public. So, for the majority of us the internet did not start to come into our lives until the 1990s.

Seemingly overnight there were hundreds of new internet-based companies that started in Silicon Valley. TV and Radio ads started giving website addresses, back when the spot would read, "go to W, W, W, dot."

In 1992 there were a total of ten websites. That number grew to 3,000 websites by 1994 and two million websites by the time Google was founded in 1998. Today there are an estimated 1.88 billion websites and growing.

Companies like Amazon, Google, and Facebook did not exist before the World Wide Web was invented. But all three have altered how we market our businesses today.

Websites are Important

IN DOING RESEARCH for this book, I was surprised to learn that less than 64 percent of small businesses have a website. This is data from 2019. If you fall into this category, let this statistic sink in: 70 to 80 percent of consumers will research a company online before they ever step foot in the door or make a purchase. How much business are you losing if you don't have a website?

Think about your own personal shopping habits. Before you try out a new restaurant or shop for a new article of clothing, do you go online and research?

If you have a website, how often do you update your content? Do you have videos on your website? Do you keep your SEO current? All these questions you need to be asking yourself. The good news is, we are going to dive into some practical tips to help you better understand what you need to market your business online.

Search Engine Optimization

SEO, OR SEARCH Engine Optimization, is how prospects organically find your website online. When you open a search engine browser, like Google, and type in a search, a list of websites come up. This is an organic search, which is different from someone going directly to your website.

SEO is about making sure your website has the proper keywords. Keywords are the words you think someone might type in when searching for the products or services you offer. They may be more like key phrases, but keywords can also be single words.

Let's say you own a hamburger restaurant in your hometown. One of the keywords would be "hamburger," but you might also list the city location of your restaurant. If someone is traveling to your hometown, they might search by city location and then the word "hamburger;" for example, "dallas texas hamburger."

But your menu might also include the best chicken sandwich in your community. If you leave out the keyword "chicken sandwich" or "best chicken sandwich," you will be losing potential customers looking for a chicken sandwich.

A friend in the business gave me the best illustration for understanding SEO. Think back to your school days when you had to write a research paper. You would go to the local library and search for a book using the Dewey Decimal System. This allowed you to search for books by author title, classification, and book title. The index cards would give you a corresponding number that would help you locate the book you were needing for your research project.

Search Engine Optimization is the Dewey Decimal System of the World Wide Web. We plug in words that we are looking for and the search engine browser pulls up websites. But what if you don't have the proper keywords on your website? How will prospects find you?

That is why you need to optimize your search results. When I talk to small business owners, I personally find most don't understand that SEO is not a one-time project. You must work on updating your SEO monthly. There are two main reasons. The first is to keep your website fresh. The second is the reality that the search engine algorithms are constantly changing.

Allow me to get a little nerdy with you. The way search engines, like Google, work is there is artificial intelligence scanning all the websites looking for keywords to put the websites into categories. The websites that are updating with fresh content get a higher priority placed over the websites that are not updated.

This may sound unfair on the surface, but small businesses shut down all the time. A static website is often an indicator that a particular establishment is no longer open for business. From a consumer stand-point, you want your Google searches to give you the best options. You don't want a search to pull up companies that are no longer open.

That means if you are busy doing what you do best, and not updating your website, you are losing potential clients.

Algorithms are a set of rules programmed by the search engines to determine which websites pull up first. Google, which owns more than 70 percent of the search engine market share, changes these algorithms often. For example, when Google purchased YouTube, the algorithm changed to make having video on your site a higher priority.

Again, on the surface this might seem a little unfair. By the time you get the algorithm down and have your website showing up on the first page of Google searches, the rules of the game change. Why? The main reason is that Google wants to make sure the searches are truly organic, and the best websites pull up with a search. If the algorithms never changed, a company could simply learn to game the system and have their website number one on the search engine, when in fact the competition might offer better reviews and services.

Bottom line, you need to keep your content fresh and update your SEO monthly. There are a lot of companies and individuals you can hire to help you with your SEO. Ask for referrals from other clients they have helped before you give someone you don't know access to your website. If you have not updated your SEO in years, be patient as this is not an overnight success. It takes time to build proper SEO, but you should start to see improvement after sixty days. There are tools available to rank your website and properly see how your SEO is working. I like using Moz.com to check websites. They offer a free tool, but you can also upgrade to get more detailed information.

Best Practices for SEO

IT IS IMPOSSIBLE for me to list all the best practices for keeping your SEO current. As I mentioned, the algorithm changes. But there are some tips you can do to help improve your website.

Keep your content fresh. Start with writing a weekly blog. When you write about topics related to your business, it includes keywords that will attract prospects to your website. For me this is more than just using keywords for the products or services you offer. I think it is equally important to write about content that your prospects are interested in. This gets back to content marketing, which we will cover in greater detail in Chapter 11.

For example, Centerpost Media offers content marketing support for small businesses. So naturally our keywords would be centered around the services we offer. I can write a blog on how to stop ignoring your social media, or how to create the perfect video for your website. But I also write about topics that our prospects are interested in, general topics related to business. I might write a blog on how to better communicate with your team or how to hire your next great talent. A prospect might find our website based on the content we are writing about on our blog and start to become familiar with the services we offer.

Blogs are the easiest way to keep your website fresh. By posting a weekly blog, you are adding content to your website. The key is to keep it updated. If you start a blog, keep writing. An old blog does the opposite. Not a writer? You can hire ghost writers to write for you. There is time you will have to spend on the front end, educating your ghost writer to understand your products or services and write in a style that matches the company's brand.

Promote the blog through your social media and email a link to the blog to your current clients. This leads to people going to your website to read the content, another bonus to boosting your SEO. Website visits play a major role in the algorithms used to determine how your website fares against the competition. Search engines are not only looking for fresh content, but they are going to promote the more popular sites first.

To that end, another key factor is backlinks. Backlinks are exactly what they sound like: links on other websites that bring people back to your website. If you can get someone else to link to your website, that helps with your SEO ranking. The key is to make sure the services are related. The more backlinks you have to your website the more popular your business appears to the algorithms. The more popular you appear, the more likely your website will show up on the first page of searches.

You might ask current clients to refer people to your website. Public Relations agencies can help get you some earned media, when news organizations will interview you about your business. Make sure the article links back to your website.

Think quality over quantity. You want backlinks that give your website authority. More backlinks are good, but you want to rank quality over quantity.

Adding video to your website is also helpful. As mentioned before, Google owns YouTube. According to Forbes, the average internet user will spend 88 percent more time on websites with video versus sites without video. That is yet another key factor to algorithms: average time spent on your website per user.

There are also monetization reasons for having video on your website. The same survey published by Forbes shows that 64 percent of internet users are more likely to make a purchase after watching a video online. And 80 percent of online guests can recall a video ad they've seen for at least thirty days.

Images on your website can also improve your SEO. Choose images that match your keywords. More than 20 percent of all web searches in the United States happen on Google Images.

Overall user experience has become an even bigger factor in algorithms. You want to make sure your website loads fast and check for any broken links on your site. A slow loading website or one filled with 404 error codes will penalize your web search.

Because algorithms change so frequently, I do recommend you hire a company to stay on top of your SEO. You can spend a lot of money on marketing and lose a ton of business because your website is not properly working or showing up in web searches. For example, if you own an AC Repair business and advertise on local TV, but your website keywords are not updated, you might be helping your competition. Have you ever watched a commercial, but could not think of the name of the business? What do you do? You enter the name of your local city and type in the service that business offers to try to locate them. Make sure your SEO is up to date.

Search Engine Marketing

You can also market your website to increase search results. This is referred to as Search Engine Marketing or SEM. You might also see SEM referred to as paid search or pay-per-click (PPC).

Do a Google search on any topic and you are likely to see a few websites listed at the top with the word "Ad" next to the result. Those companies have paid to have their websites listed on the front page.

This is a cost-effective way to market your business because you only pay when a prospect clicks on your website. You do not have to pay for your website showing up on the list, only when the prospect clicks on the ad.

You are also marketing to prospects who are more likely to be ready to make a purchase. If someone is doing a web search for wedding cakes, and you own a bakery that specializes in cakes, you want that prospect visiting your website instead of your competitor's site.

We will discuss SEM in more detail, including some resources for you to get started, in Chapter Nine when we dive into digital marketing.

Google Analytics

ONE OF THE first questions I ask small business owners I meet is if they have set up their Google Analytics on their website. Most just give me a blank stare. If that describes you, take comfort that you are not alone and be encouraged that this section will give you some free practical advice to help your business.

For starters, Google Analytics is free. So, everything I am about to describe to you can be set up by you or someone on your team at no charge. If you are using Google Analytics already, I will offer you some tips that you might consider tweaking if you have not already done so.

What is Google Analytics? Google launched this service in 2005 to help website owners track how people are interacting with their site. You can see in real time how many people are on your website, where in the world they are located, what the demographics are, how they found your website, what they do once they are on your site, and if their visit leads to a sale.

I run a small business, so I knew I wanted to make sure our websites were working properly. The way my mind works, I don't just want to know the how, I want to know the why. So, I got Google Analytics Certified by taking their free online Google Analytics for Beginners and the free online Advanced Google Analytics courses. Sounds impressive, but my point is that you can do the same today. I completed both courses in less than a week and updated our websites in the process.

I have mentioned before that everything in the digital space is trackable. Your computer has an IP address that is associated with your location. When you go to a website, that site knows that your IP address is visiting. It knows if you are a first-time visitor or a repeat visitor. There is a lot that is known about you based on where you live. This includes your demographics. Google also knows your search history and based on that history Google knows what you are interested in and how likely you are ready to make a purchase.

I joke that Google probably knows more about me than I know about myself. And all this information might freak you out if you didn't already know that you have a digital fingerprint online. I confess after I learned about Google Analytics, I started using a different search engine for searches related to personal information, like medical questions. I noticed that some of our website visitor's information on Google Analytics was hidden from a search engine that I had never heard of before my research. If you want to personally search without your information being shared, stop using Google and start using DuckDuckGo. Your information is still being tracked, but DuckDuckGo does not share details with other websites.

But there is a benefit to having your likes and interests tracked. Google is trying to recommend websites and products that you are interested in. Yes, Google is a business, and they are monetizing from your searches, but there is a reason that Google owns more than 70 percent of the market share. Google is good. I have typed in a search in DuckDuckGo and not found what I was looking for, because the algorithms are different. So, I use both depending on what I am searching for.

The first thing you need to do is sign up for a free account by going to analytics.google.com. You will need a Google Account, so if you do not already have a Gmail address you will need to set one up. I recommend you set up a separate Gmail account to track your company's website analytics. This will most likely be information that is shared with other members of your team in the future, so you don't want to tie your company's Google Analytics account with a personal Gmail.

Once you complete the set-up process, you can add multiple websites to your Google Analytics page. Each website will be assigned a tracking ID that starts with "UA." This is how Google will start to share information specific to your website. Each website has its own unique tracking ID number. Your webmaster will need to place this tracking ID on the website. This is done in the coding of your website. Unless you know computer coding, it's best to have an expert add the tracking ID.

Remember earlier when we discussed the artificial intelligence that tracks websites? Those are often referred to as "bots." The bots can skew your data, making it appear like you have more visitors to your website than you do. You can fine tune your search to remove the bots and other white noise, so that you are only tracking human interactivity.

From there you can start to create custom reports to track the data that is more important to your business. I like to track the audience's age and gender. This gives me information about our target demographic for our services. You might be surprised to learn that your actual demographic looks a little different than who you thought you were reaching. This could lead to a change in your overall marketing strategy or some changes to your site to better attract the right demographics.

I also want to know where my website visitors are located. I run a national business, so for me that is important to know. If you are local only, you might want to track location to only look at the data from your market.

I look at the audience interests to get an idea what my website visitors are searching online. This gives me a snapshot of what they are most interested in and I then compare it with how it aligns with the products and services we offer. For example, it makes sense that one of the top interests for visitors to BizTalkRadio.com is banking and financial advice. Our content aligns with what our website visitors want to consume.

As a media company, I also use those interests to better understand what types of commercials would get the best results on our properties. "Food and Dining" shows up as an interest, so running a national advertisement for a restaurant makes sense. I can also run Google ads on my website for additional revenue. Google will place ads related to audience interest.

The Audience Market Category is similar, but Google has identified these searches as someone who is ready to make a purchase now. Where interest could be an ongoing interest, the market category is someone looking to spend money. Again, no surprise that BizTalkRadio.com shows its top market category is Financial Services. Visitors to that website are looking to hire someone to help them manage their money.

Digging deeper into the audience numbers, I am looking to see how many users are coming to our websites. Of the total users, how many are new and how many are returning visitors. I want new visitors, but a higher percentage of returning visitors lets me know we are offering something of value. Continuing to use BizTalkRadio as an example, 78 percent of our website visitors are repeat businesses. In our case we offer a stream of our radio network and past episodes all posted for free.

Users equal the total number of unique visitors to your website. Again, this is based on IP address. It's possible one user could log on to your website at home and then log on to your website using a different device at the office. That one user would be counted as two users.

Sessions equal the number of visits a user makes to your website. One user can come to your website multiple times. That user would be counted as one unique user, but each session would be counted separately. A single session can have multiple page views.

Sessions are tracked by using internet cookies. Cookies are information saved by your web browser. Every time someone visits your website, their web browser gives them a cookie. Yum! Cookies are good; they are how you can save passwords and information that help you navigate websites more easily on the second visit.

The flipside of that is users can clear the cookies after each website visit. That means when they return to your website, the Google Analytics data will treat them like a new visitor to the website.

There are more details you can dig into, like average session duration, which is how long they are staying on your website, and the number of sessions per user or pages per session average.

You also want to look at the bounce rate of your website. This is the percentage of visitors who go to a specific page and then leave your site before clicking on any other pages.

Pageviews are self-explanatory; this is the number of page views during the selected time frame. If a user refreshes the page during a session, that will be counted as an additional pageview.

Under "Acquisition Data" you can start to track how people are visiting your website. Are they going directly to your website, meaning they are typing in your address? Or are they coming to your website via a referral? These are the backlinks from other websites. You can also track organic search when people are finding your website via a Google search. Finally, you can see how people are coming to your website via your social media channels.

This is all great information to know; which of your marketing campaigns are working? If you are paying for SEM, but not seeing results on the organic search, you need to consider tweaking your campaign. Same with social media. If you are paying for social media marketing, but not seeing results from social media, tweak your campaign.

Under "Behavior Data" you can see where visitors to your website are going. This data lets you know what information is important to your customers and prospects. It might lead you to offering more of the services they are checking out on a particular page or creating an ad you place on the popular pages to try to get users to visit other pages on your website.

On "Conversions," you can set up campaigns that you can track on your website. If you have a shopping cart, you could set up a campaign that tracks users who land on the shopping cart page. This data will show you what pages the users visited before landing on the shopping cart, and you can even track if they made a purchase or not.

This is great information if you are looking to improve the customer experience. If you notice a high bounce rate in one area of the process, you can start to analyze reasons. Perhaps it's the price point page, so your product might be priced too high. It could be something as simple as a webpage that is not working properly or is not user-friendly.

Can you see how all this data could help you with your business?

Conclusion

WE LIVE IN a digital world, and you need to have a website that is easy to find and easy to use to be competitive in today's business environment.

It is not enough to have a website; you need to make sure your Search Engine Optimization is up-to-date. There are several things you can start doing yourself today, but consider hiring a professional company that keeps current with the latest Google Algorithm updates.

You can purchase Search Engine Marketing to help your website get noticed faster; more details in Chapter Nine.

Finally, if you have not done so already, set up Google Analytics. It is free and you will start to learn a lot about your current and prospective clients. Understanding the demographics you reach will help any marketing campaign you are considering. Before you purchase a radio or TV ad, buy a print ad, a programmatic ad, or start a digital campaign, know your demographics. Google Analytics is a great resource for learning this information.

8

SOCIAL MEDIA

DON'T RECALL the exact date someone first told me about Myspace, but I remember thinking it was just another Classmates.com. The idea of tracking down old high school friends and seeing how their lives turned out seemed of interest to me for all of about one evening. I went online and created a profile and started searching for names from my past. Then I pretty much forgot about having an account and moved on with my life.

Okay, so I checked on my profile a couple of times after creating it, but it was not a great experience. My career moved me to Atlanta in 2007 and I think the last thing I posted on my profile was Ray Charles' song, "Georgia On My Mind." Once we moved into our new home and I started my new job, we found out my wife was pregnant with our youngest daughter and life got busy.

The following year I was introduced to Facebook, which I joined in March of 2008. The experience was different. Finding old friends was easier and seeing pictures of their families was fun. Most of our extended family and friends still lived in Texas, so Facebook gave us an outlet to keep up with them online.

My first status update was submitting the day I was born, followed by when I graduated from high school and college. But the first update I ever typed was, "Off to New York on a business trip." I am sure all my friends and family's day was improved by knowing I was going to New York. Or my favorite early posts where I told the world I was off to eat lunch or that I was answering emails.

I joined Twitter in September of 2008, which really got me into microblogging my day. It is so funny to think back on how we all viewed social media in the early days.

I caught a panel discussion of former staff who worked under George W. Bush on CSPAN a few years ago. It was a fascinating dive into how the White House had to adapt to using social media in the middle of the administration. Bush was elected President in 2000, before Myspace, Facebook, and Twitter. He was reelected in 2004 when social media was just starting to take off, and by the time Bush left office his successor, President Barack Obama, used social media to raise money for his campaign and grassroots marketing.

Leave no doubt that social media has changed our culture in both positive and negative ways. Stories of lost loved ones connecting and people finding meaningful relationships warm our hearts. But stories of governments that have been overthrown and misinformation that cause confusion and worse, the loss of life, break our hearts.

As business owners and entrepreneurs, we can harness the power of social media to connect with our clients and prospective clients and drive results. But if we are not careful, social media can also destroy our brand with one wrong post or comment online.

History of Social Media

BEFORE THERE WAS Mark Zuckerberg there was Andrew Weinreich. In 1997, Weinreich launched SixDegrees.com, the first social media website. Playing off the concept that we are all six degrees of separation from each other, the site allowed users to list their friends, family, and people they knew and invite others to do the same. Once you confirmed your relationship, you could send messages and post items on a virtual bulletin board. You can still go to SixDegrees.com today, but the service ended in the year 2000.

In 2001 Friendster was launched with a similar idea of connecting users for basic online networking. We might still be using Friendster today, had the founders not turned down an offer by Google for thirty million dollars in 2003, a decision considered one of the biggest blunders in Silicon Valley. In 2011, the site was repositioned as a social gaming site, but shut down completely in 2018.

Reid Hoffman founded LinkedIn in 2002 and launched the site in 2003. By August of 2004, LinkedIn had one million users. Microsoft acquired LinkedIn in January of 2017 and today there are more than 774 million registered members in more than 200 countries or territories worldwide.

The forementioned Myspace launched in 2003 and became the most visited website globally by 2006, when users could share new music on the platform. News Corp., the parent company to FOX News, owned the site from 2005 to 2011, when Justin Timberlake purchased Myspace for $35 million, and today you can log on and find and follow your favorite music artist. But the site really is an afterthought. The copyright year on the website is listed as 2014, which is a good indicator the site is not being fully maintained.

In 2004, Mark Zuckerberg and a few of his Harvard College roommates launched Facebook, named after the directories given to university students with classmates' pictures. Initially, membership was limited to Harvard students, and then offered to other universities. In 2006, Facebook opened to anyone aged thirteen and older.

Other popular social media sites followed. Twitter launched in 2006. Google has tried to get into the social space several times over the years. Their most successful attempt was Google+, launched in 2011, but was discontinued in 2019. Instagram and Pinterest both launched in 2010. Snapchat started in 2011 and TikTok in 2016.

According to Pew Research Center, 72 percent of adults in the United States use some form of social media. That is up from only 5 percent of adults in 2005.

In 2010, I took a job with a technology company that was experimenting with the concept of integrating social media into a linear TV network. The idea was to allow viewers of Youtoo TV to create "famespots," which were thirty-second video spots, and submit the content to air on national TV. Our team created a process where someone could record a video in response to a question and be on television within two minutes of submitting the spot. Ultimately the concept failed because TV viewers are looking for a "lean-back" experience, meaning they want to relax and be entertained when watching television, not create a spot and see themselves on TV. Although we did receive a lot of interesting videos from average Americans, some of which we could not air on TV.

I learned a lot about social media during my time at Youtoo. In our research we noticed a pattern with all social media platforms. The early adopters are almost always college age students, followed by high school and junior high kids. The data showed the younger kids learned about the new social media from siblings in college. Once the teenagers were online with a new platform, mom and dad would join. Then after the parents were active on the platform, the grandparents became aware, and the college kids were already off to the next social media platform.

In the Miller house, we didn't allow our girls to get on social media until they were in high school and even then, it was very limited. But when our first born was old enough to get social media, I offered to help her sign up on Facebook. By then she couldn't care less about Facebook and was only interested in Instagram, TikTok, and Snapchat.

This is a good data point to keep in mind when you are looking at what social media platforms to have a presence on with your brand. What are the demographics you are trying to reach? Match those demographics with the social media platform that makes the most sense.

Facebook and Instagram

THERE HAS BEEN a lot written about the downfall of Facebook, and there is no doubt Facebook has some branding issues to overcome. But numbers don't lie, and the data shows that more than 2.8 billion people use the platform every single month. Hootsuite, a social media management tool, reports that two-thirds of Facebook users say they visit a local business Facebook page at least once a week. So how can you use Facebook to promote your business?

For starters, if you have not already done so, create a page for your business. Setting up a Facebook page is free. You can post information about your business, like when you are open, a link to your website, contact information, and even sell products directly from your page, all at no cost.

Make sure you choose a custom username that will help people find you. Most likely this will be your business name, but you might have to get creative if your name is already taken. An example might be adding your local city in front of your business name. Consider also creating a public figure page for yourself if you are the founder or leader of your company. Marketing yourself is equally important to marketing your company. Again, choose a custom username that makes it easy for people to find you. I have a very common name, there are thousands of Scott Millers, and surprisingly a lot of us are CEOs. I chose @scottmillerceo for my social username. It is easy to remember and easy to find. And your profile name is searchable online.

Facebook will prompt you with ways to maximize your page, so follow the directions and don't be afraid to go back and review and make edits on your page.

Did you know that Facebook is ranked as the fourth most popular site for internet searches? It's true, Facebook is behind only Google, YouTube, and Amazon in internet searches. If you don't have a Facebook page, you are losing potential business.

Facebook also owns Instagram, so if you are going to have both a Facebook and Instagram page, or if you end up with multiple Facebook pages to manage, open a Facebook Business Suite account. There is a separate app and desktop website for Facebook Business Suite. This will allow you to schedule future posts, stories, and ads for your company. You can also respond to comments and messages sent to your accounts. This service is also free.

Insights is a great tool to show you how your Facebook or Instagram pages are performing. Here you can check out your overall reach in a selected time frame. You can also see what posts are outperforming the others to get ideas for future posts. And you can see demographic information about your followers. I like to compare these data points with what we are seeing on Google Analytics. This lets me know if our social media brand is consistent with our overall brand.

I am big on understanding what demographics you are trying to reach. When I meet with a small business to discuss marketing, that is always the first question I ask, "Tell me who your ideal customer is." When you get into Facebook marketing, it is important to know who you are trying to reach.

There are other features you can explore in your Facebook Business Suite. It is important to know that Facebook wants your page to be successful. Their goal is to get as many followers on their site for as long as possible, so Facebook wants to help you maximize your page. Pay close attention to the tips that Facebook gives you as you build out your page.

Instagram was purchased by Facebook in April of 2012 for one billion in cash and stock. Where Facebook allows you to post text, videos, and pictures, Instagram is a purely visual platform. Users post images or short videos. You can also post longer videos via Instagram Video.

You need a strategy for all your social media platforms, but even more so for Instagram. It's not enough to just post random pictures or videos. Again, social media is an extension of your overall brand. In this case it's about using high quality images or videos to convey your brand. The most popular Instagram accounts also coordinate their pages to be aesthetically pleasing. So that a row or rows of post have a similar color scheme or theme, for example. I want to be clear that styles change, so it is altogether possible that you will start to see a different approach to Instagram.

Having an Instagram for your business is not a requirement, in my opinion. Perhaps you create an account to reserve your name for future use, but you don't update it that often. Most social media experts agree that you do not need to worry about keeping up with every single social media platform for your business.

I have an Instagram account, @scottmillerceo if you want to follow me, but that is not my main source of business. I mainly have an account to keep up with trends to help our clients. Because my clients are business owners, I get more leads from LinkedIn. But my wife started an in-home cookie business and Instagram was a great resource for leads. She would post images of her latest cookie designs and it would prompt followers to reach out and book an order. So, give some consideration to your brand before spending too much time on Instagram. If you are selling products that you can showcase with high quality images, then you should consider that platform.

Boosting posts will get you more engagements on both platforms. Facebook is a business, and they will limit your social media if you do not spend some dollars. I recommend you start with a small budget. Spend $1 a day for thirty days and see what kind of results you get from the boost. The great part of advertising on Facebook is how detailed you can get with the target demographic. I had a client who owned a wedding chapel in Las Vegas. We boosted a post to include cities within a short flight to Vegas, and we were able to select women who are currently shopping for wedding venues. Yep, everything you search for online is stored data. But this is a good option for small businesses with small marketing budgets.

Twitter

PERSONALLY, TWITTER IS where I go to keep up with my favorite sports teams. When I am watching a game on TV, I like to see what various sports writers and fans are saying about the game. It is like being at the sports bar with random strangers without ever having to leave my house. It is also a unique platform to follow famous people you admire who share a microblog of their day. All that is great, but how do you market your business on Twitter?

If you are the founder or leader of your company, having a public twitter account makes sense. But I strongly caution you about what you share online. It doesn't matter if you delete a tweet, once online it is always online. Someone will take a screenshot or find a way to access an archive. Too many business leaders have decided to use this platform to share unfiltered thoughts and it has done more damage than helped their brand.

From a company standpoint, for Twitter to work you must find your brand's voice. Think of your business twitter account as an individual, not as a company. Wendy's does an excellent job at making people feel like they are following a person, rather than a company. Their bio says it all: "We like our tweets the way we like our fries: hot, crispy, and better than anyone expects from a fast food restaurant." The social media team at Wendy's are constantly tweeting snarky comments to their competition. For example, McDonald's sent out a tweet that read, "If u were the person who ran the McDonald's account for a day, what would u tweet." To which Wendy's shared with the reply, "Where the things that should be fresh are frozen, and the things that should be frozen are out of order."

It is always important to be true to your brand, but even more so on Twitter. You will become a trending topic in a negative way if people feel you are being inauthentic.

Twitter has a mob or herd mentality, where a group of people who might ordinarily be polite in person turn into mean people who don't mind telling you their opinions. Tread lightly!

The use of hashtags was first introduced by Twitter. Adding the "#" sign in front of a word or sentence is how you can make your tweet searchable and add to the conversation on a trending topic. All social media platforms use the hashtag now. Chris Messina first proposed the idea in a 2007 tweet. He should have patented the idea.

You can purchase promoted tweets on Twitter to get your brand in front of more people. I have seen this work for important announcements, but again you have to be careful on this platform. Promote your tweets too much and users will block your ad and if they are following your Twitter, they may get frustrated to the point of unfollowing you.

The nature of Twitter has also become somewhat toxic for brands. In the 2020 Presidential Election, President Donald Trump famously used the platform to call out his opponents or anyone who disagreed with him politically. Twitter executives felt like the President's tweets were spreading misinformation post-election and made the bold move to permanently ban the outgoing President, who at the time had 88.9 million followers. This only added fuel to the fire and made it harder for brands to associate with Twitter.

I don't think Twitter is going away anytime soon. Nestle spent $13 million dollars in Q1 of 2020 on Twitter, so it clearly works for some brands. Like all social media, proceed with caution.

Snapchat and TikTok

THE BASIC PREMISE to Snapchat is users connect with each other and "Snap" a picture or video that is sent through the app to one or more friends. The videos can only be a maximum of ten seconds long. The Snaps are deleted once viewed by all the recipients. That is unless it is shared in the users' Story, in which case the image or video will disappear after twenty-four hours. Unopened Snaps will disappear after thirty days.

How do you use Snapchat for your business? Keep in mind, social platforms have one goal, to keep users on their app as long as possible. Snapchat is appealing to the younger demographics; 82 percent of all Snapchat users are thirty-four years old or younger. If that is your target demo, you have a captive audience you can reach.

Forbes research shows that users on this platform are 60 percent more likely to make an impulsive purchase. The layout of Snapchat is business friendly with the "Discover" icon. Brands that create content specifically for Snapchat can be discovered by users of the app.

Unlike Instagram, Snapchat is about posting content that is casual and fun, not polished. You still need to be true to your brand. Don't be the mom who tries to act cool around her teenage daughters. It doesn't work.

You can set up a Snapchat Business account which gives you more options and control over your brand.

TikTok is similar, in that you create short videos, but different in that you post those videos for all your followers to see, and the videos do not disappear like Snapchat. It was created to be an outlet for young people to showcase their talent. If you want the world to see you sing, dance, lip-sync, or act out a comedy bit, then TikTok is for you. The videos can be addicting. The average time kids spend on TikTok is twenty hours a month, compared to Facebook at sixteen hours a month.

Businesses can purchase branded TikTok content to users on the platform, most of whom are under the age of nineteen. I don't have a TikTok account, but the TikTok videos have seemingly taken over other social media platforms like Facebook and Instagram.

Nextdoor

NEXTDOOR IS A crowdsourcing social media app for everything you need locally. Need someone to mow your yard, paint your house, or ideas for new restaurants? Just make a post on Nextdoor asking for recommendations. You can find a lot of helpful information from crowdsourcing your questions.

From a business standpoint, you can create an account and interact with people who live near your location. You can also become a neighborhood sponsor, which allows you to share your expertise on ideas related to your products or services, answer questions from neighbors as the business, and engage the community by posting questions to get people thinking about your brand.

Yelp

WE WILL COVER Yelp in more detail later when we discuss how to make sure your business is properly listed. Yelp is an app and, like Nextdoor, users crowdsource information about local businesses. But I view Yelp more like a modern Yellow Pages, so we will cover how to use Yelp in Chapter Ten.

LinkedIn

IF YOU ARE looking for your next great career or are marketing to businesses, chances are you have been on LinkedIn. This is the social media platform for the business professional. Users post content related to their job or work in general.

It is important that you keep your professional profile up to date, as the content on LinkedIn is available for public searching. Some information is hidden, but if I know where you are located or where you work, I can most likely find your LinkedIn profile. This is true even when I am not signed into LinkedIn, though some information is hidden when not connected. This is what a lot of companies do to research prospective new hires. If you open a web browser not logged into your LinkedIn account, you can view people's pages without their knowledge. Along those same lines, anything you post on social media that is public could be viewed by prospective clients. Keep that in mind when making posts, even on your personal accounts.

LinkedIn is a great resource for potential clients to discover you and your business if you know how to maximize your page. That is far more impactful than using LinkedIn for cold calling. First, I hope after you read this book you will see that a strong marketing plan is far more effective than just picking up the phone or sending someone an email. As the CEO of a company, I lose count of the number of people who want to connect with me just to sell me their product or service. Please stop, there is a better way. I want to show you how to build trust with prospects first, so they will come to you when they need your services.

The first thing you want to do is create a public profile URL that is unique to you. Click on your profile and then click "edit public profile & URL." This is where you can create a searchable URL that helps people find you. Don't just use your name, include a word that describes what you do. As an example, my URL is www.linkedin.com/in/scottmiller-media. Google Scott Miller media and you will likely find my LinkedIn profile on the first page of the Google search. If I meet someone, and they cannot remember the name of my company, but they remember my name and that I work in media, they can find me. The default will be your name, followed by some numbers. No one will search those numbers.

Next, use the Headline option to give prospects more information than just where you work. The Headline is part of what is searchable online, so you can describe some of the services you offer, or highlight what makes you different from your peers. My Headline showcases that in addition to being the CEO of Centerpost Media, I host the "Create. Build. Manage." show and am an author. I list that I am a member of the Forbes Agency Council, Entrepreneur Leadership Network and the Dallas Business Journal Leadership Trust. Finally, I list that I help businesses with content marketing. All these things let prospects know that I have credibility and that I can help them with specific services.

You also want to make sure you have a professional profile picture on LinkedIn and use the cover photo to help explain what you do through imagery. You do not want a picture with your significant other, your kids, or your pets. Remember, LinkedIn is for professional networking.

Your "About" section is also available to people not connected with you and is searchable online. Use keywords that you want to be discoverable. I also recommend you use this space to give contact information. The "Contact info" link is only available to people already connected to you. In my case I have my assistant's email listed if someone wants to book a meeting, and my PR Agent's contact if someone from the media wants to interview me. Why lose out on potential business because we are not connected on LinkedIn?

Because I help small businesses with content marketing, I have "Creator Mode" turned on on my profile. This allows me to highlight a few videos or posts at the top of my page.

When you are updating your "Experience" section on LinkedIn, write in the first person. Imagine you are introducing yourself to someone for the first time. I wouldn't say, "Mr. Miller was named CEO of Centerpost Media in July of 2020." Instead, if I met you in person and you asked about my job I might say, "I was named CEO of Centerpost Media in July of 2020."

Make sure your company has a public LinkedIn page. This will allow you to connect your experience to the company page and include a company logo. You are more likely to get discovered before your company, and this will give prospects a natural flow to finding out more information on your business. This is particularly important if you are marketing to businesses.

You can include your education and any honors and awards you have received or been a part of in your career. Finally, you can ask current and former clients to leave you a recommendation or ask current and former colleagues to do the same. This is another way for prospects to get to know you.

You can advertise on LinkedIn. Promoted posts get your brand in front of prospects who are not following you. I find spending dollars on job openings to be an effective way to get our brand out in front of prospects. It shows that we are a growing company, and it's a nice way of marketing the company without looking like we are marketing the company. Bonus, you pull in more qualified candidates for the job.

When we discuss content marketing in detail, I will show you how to create engaging posts that get prospects reaching out to you.

The one drawback to LinkedIn is how people connect with the platform. Most use a personal email address, instead of a professional one.

I do find this challenging when engaging with prospects who reach out to me. They are interested, but the notifications that I have responded to their message often go unseen for days, sometimes weeks. They are landing in an unread inbox. Another reason cold call messages on LinkedIn do not work. A good reminder that if you are going to use LinkedIn for work, connect a professional email address or at least make sure it is an email address you check frequently so you do not miss important messages.

Emerging Platforms

IT IS IMPOSSIBLE to list all the potential social media platforms in print. Clubhouse took off during the pandemic to fill the void of not being able to network in person. I don't see this as being a viable platform for small businesses. I have met a couple of people who were early adopters and they found new clients and made some money. The problem is, to hit their level of success, they were on the platform for several hours a day and on weekends. I don't know a lot of small business owners who have that kind of time available.

With any new platform, remember that most start with college age students, move to teenagers, then parents, and finally grandparents. Take the time to understand the demographics any new platform reaches and see if it is a match to your target demo. Do some research by looking at major brands who are using the platform. They have big marketing budgets that include research. Learn from their knowledge.

How to Use Social Media

IF YOU ALREADY have one or more of these platforms, how are they working for you? Most small businesses I talk to have created social media accounts and they see the value in having a presence on social media, but they really don't know where to begin on getting the platform to work for them.

Let's first discuss the difference between social media interactions and monetizing your social media. Social interactions are the likes, shares, and comments you get from your posts. Monetizing is when you turn those interactions into clients who pay you for your products or services.

Most small businesses get caught up in the interactions and lose sight of monetizing. If you want more likes on your posts, share images or videos of babies or pets. Who doesn't love a cute baby or puppy? You can also post funny memes to get people laughing and liking. But do those posts translate to money for your business? Unless you own a pet store, cute kittens are not going to lead to more sales. There is not an equal equation of social interactions to monetization.

What should you be sharing on your social media? Social media needs to be an extension of your brand. Would you post cute baby pictures on your company website? Probably not, unless you owned a clothing resale shop that included baby clothes. But you would post information related to your products. That needs to be the focus of your social media strategy.

Do not get sucked into following the latest social media trends unless the trend is on point with your brand. In 2015, there was a great debate over the color of a particular dress. You either saw the dress as black and blue or white and gold. To me it looked more brown and blue, but millions of us weighed in on the topic.

When President Joe Biden was inaugurated in January of 2021, it was a cold day in Washington. Photojournalist Brendan Smialowski snapped a picture of Vermont Senator Bernie Sanders wearing a mask, oversized mittens, and a brown coat, sitting in a folding chair with his legs and arms crossed. His image quickly went viral with people photoshopping Bernie's image in all kinds of places. The Senator was on the moon, in coffee shops, and on t-shirts you could purchase online. I confess, we joined in on the fun and had Bernie sitting on-set of one of our local TV shows being interviewed.

But the trends do not lead to new business. Not a single person reached out to us after we posted our Bernie picture and said, "Hey,

I saw that fun picture of Bernie Sanders you posted on Facebook, do you think you can help me market my business?"

If the trend is on point with your brand, you should consider having some fun. If you own a clothing store, using the dress would have been a golden opportunity to remind people that you sell dresses.

Is posting fun images hurtful to your brand? Not necessarily, but I am really addressing those small businesses whose only social media strategy is to wait for the next big trending topic and then posting about it on their business page.

Do you have a marketing strategy laid out for the year? If you do, then your social media should follow that strategy. If you don't, then now is the time to start to think about what a marketing strategy would look like for your business.

Here are some practical tips to consider. Look at your previous profit and loss statements. What do they tell you about your business? You have times of the year where you sell certain types of products. There are slow times in your business cycle. Those are data points to help you strategize your marketing plan. You might promote those hot ticket items to drive more sales, or you might push those products in the slow cycles to increase your bottom-line.

Use a holiday calendar to think about how the different seasons relate to your products or services. Do you sell more during the holiday shopping season, or is your busy time after your customers get their income tax checks back?

Finally, think about what your repeat business or prospects are thinking about when planning out your marketing strategy. Your demographics might be adults in their thirties and forties who have kids at home. If that is the case your target demo is thinking about spring break, summer vacations, back to school, and winter break. What kind of planned messages can you create to meet your prospects where they are, tapping into their mindset?

Once you have analyzed all the data, create a year-long calendar for your social posts. Then you can start to get ahead and create graphics, cool images, videos, and wordsmith your posts. You can use tools to pre schedule posts each month based on your calendar. This still leaves room for you to react to any trending topic that fits your brand.

One word of caution: never leave your social media on autopilot. You need to know what posts are coming up to make any necessary changes. One of our TV hosts told me a story about a music festival she was organizing when the artist Prince died. They canceled the original post planned and instead sent out a post dedicated to Prince.

You also want to make sure you are responding to likes and comments online, even the negative ones. You would not leave a prospect sitting in your lobby for days, so don't leave a comment unanswered.

Conclusion

THERE IS MORE we can learn about social media. Unlike print or broadcasting, the platforms are still new and evolving quickly. It is important to have a presence on social media, but pick the platforms that best fit your target demographic.

Above all, be proactive and not just reactive on social media. Having a plan and using social media to be an extension of your brand will be far more successful in the long run than worrying about trends and likes and comments. Social engagement is good, it helps you extend your brand, but most important is bringing in new clients. Choose content that draws in your prospects to do business with you.

Remember when we discussed Google Analytics in the previous chapter? Check to see if you are getting leads from your social media. That is a great indicator of the efficiency of your strategy.

9

DIGITAL MARKETING

IT IS HARD to imagine what life was like before we were all digitally connected, but there existed a world before smartphones and the ability to Google anything. One of my long-standing jokes with my family is when one of them will ask me a question that I don't know the answer to. My response is always the same: "If only they invented a device where we can search for the answer."

Think about how attached you are to your smartphone. My iPhone gives me a weekly report to remind me just how many hours we spent together. Thanks Apple.

Like all great inventions, there is the good and the bad. I love the ability to stay connected with family and friends. I am a naturally curious person, so I enjoy pulling out my phone to research a thought process. But I confess, I miss the days of not being connected. When my dad left his store, he didn't think about work unless they called the home phone line with an urgent need. He was home, spending time with us kids. Not the case in my generation. I get emails and text messages that remind me of work around the clock.

My first smartphone was a Blackberry Curve. I had never heard of text messaging before my job issued me my phone. I confess, I was addicted. Around the office we called it our "crack-berry" because we all loved the ability to stay connected. I remember standing in line at Disney with my wife, four-year-old, and baby and answering a work text message.

One day at home after a twelve-hour workday, I was on my phone answering an email when my wife politely asked, "Do you think when you are home, you can actually be home with us?" Ouch. That was my wake-up call. I started a new habit that day of plugging my smartphone in and leaving it to charge when I got home and spending time with the family.

I recently went on a vacation with my family to Hawaii. I turned off all email and Skype notifications and just unplugged. I still checked into the office a couple of times; as CEO it's part of the job, but it was on my timeline. When I got back to the office, I never turned the notifications back on and it was the best decision I ever made related to my smartphone. I am one of those people that if I see unread emails, I have to check them. Today it looks like I don't have any unread emails. Only when I open my email app do I see the unread emails. What's amazing is I have not missed anything. I still get my emails answered, and I am less stressed.

That's my story, but the reality is I am not alone. More and more people are constantly connected and checking email, reading text messages, and searching online for information about products and services they want to purchase. Everything in the digital world is trackable and we all have a digital fingerprint that companies can use to market to us. What exactly do companies know about us? Is technology listening to our conversations? How can you as a business owner take advantage of digital data to market to your prospects? Let's unpack these questions and give you some practical tips to improve your digital marketing strategy.

What is Digital Marketing?

DIGITAL MARKETING IS any promotion of products and services that utilizes connected devices and electronic media, whether it's smartphones, computers, set top devices, or anything else connected with internet access.

Digital Marketing includes the emails you receive from the store you visited, the suggested websites at the top of a Google search, ads you see online and on social media, text messages from companies, social media promotions, video content pushed out, and that celebrity you love to follow on Twitter who just mentioned a product they enjoy.

An advertiser's dream is to be able to reach the ideal prospect for brand awareness and stay connected to the point of making a purchasing decision. When you, as a consumer, go online and search for a product or service, that is data that can be used by an advertiser to market their company to you. For some, this is creepy. And companies like Apple are aware of a growing concern of just how much data is being shared with advertisers. A recent update on my smartphone shows me how many times Apple is blocking a website from tracking my online searches. This is important to keep note of, as the world of digital marketing is going to change.

What data is being shared with advertisers? This is a great question and worth unpacking. For starters, in the digital world you don't have a name and home address. Instead, you have a device and an IP address. Your device is whatever you use to connect to the internet. Your IP address is your Internet Protocol, the unique set of numbers that identifies your device on the internet.

At home or at the office, when you are connected to the internet, your provider has assigned a range of IP numbers that are unique to that location. If you are curious, Google "what is my IP address" and you can see what set of numbers are connected to your device. You cannot access the internet without an IP address.

Another way to look at an IP address is comparing it to a phone number. You cannot call someone without a phone number. Before the internet and mobile phones, you had a landline. Remember the telemarketing calls you got in the middle of dinner? Businesses would staff call centers to market to you at home. Did they know where you lived? Yes. Each phone number has an area code, and that code is specific to your location. And it would not take a lot of research to pinpoint your exact address. The phone company published a list of everyone's phone number and gave that information away to everyone.

In that sense digital marketing is not all that different from telemarketing, only now advertisers are not calling you during dinner; instead they are targeting messages online. Where it gets to be different is what information they know about you. Back in the landline days, advertisers did not know who you were calling or what stores you were visiting or what you circled in the catalog that came in the mail. Today, all that information is known.

To be clear, an advertiser cannot purchase a list of names with information about what people are searching for online. Again, you are just a device and an IP address. But let's be honest, your phone provider, phone manufacturer, and internet search engine have that information. They are just not passing that information on to advertisers. If you picked up a landline phone and dialed 911 today, the police would know your exact address. If you use "find a friend" tracking on your mobile devices and know exactly where your friends and family are, guess what, the phone company also knows. That is why it is important that these companies keep this information private.

Do companies like Amazon, Facebook, and Google listen to our conversations? Have you ever had a discussion with someone about a topic, and later you see an ad pop up on Facebook about the same topic? Real creepy. Facebook has denied eavesdropping in on your conversations and there is likely a logical reason that has happened to you.

When you visit a website, that site will place "cookies" on your device. Those cookies help gather information about your time on the website and if you revisit the site later. But they can also be used to remarket to you. You might not have researched the topic you were discussing with your friend, but they could have after your conversation. If you are on the same internet network, you might see that ad later. Or Facebook is not telling us the truth and they are listening in on our conversations. I will let you decide. But I can tell you that you cannot purchase that kind of information as an advertiser.

Amazon and Google are listening to your conversations if you have an Alexa or Google Home device. The way those devices work is to listen for the keyword to wake it up and answer your question. "Alexa" or "Hey Google" will prompt the smart device to hear your question and then answer it accordingly. I saw a funny internet meme that showed the difference in America between the 1950s and today. One image showed a housewife in the 1950s talking on a landline saying, "Be quiet, the government might be listening." The other image showed a woman today asking her Alexa device, "Hey government, what is a good tuna casserole recipe?"

Is digital marketing good or bad? That really is based on your perspective. My kids have grown up in a world where there never was privacy, so their generation does not expect privacy. Think about it, we shared baby pictures and precious moments of their lives on social media. They are always connected with everyone at their schools. This is the world they grew up in. My parents' generation is the opposite. They hate the idea of being tracked online and want more privacy. For me, I am in the middle. I like the fact that I get ads that are relative to me. I don't mind being marketed products or services that I either need or desire. At the same time, I feel there is information that needs to remain private. I believe we have a moral responsibility as businesses to market to prospects in a healthy way, without violating people's privacy.

History of Digital Marketing

THE TERM "DIGITAL MARKETING" was coined in the late 1990s when the internet was just starting to take off. Prior to 1994, getting on the internet was challenging. Netscape Navigator was the first commercial web browser that launched in October of that year, making it easier for people to search and find websites.

AT&T purchased the first banner ad two weeks later on the website HotWired.com. The ad was part of an overall marketing campaign titled "You Will." The banner ad did not mention AT&T, it simply read, "Have you ever clicked your mouse right HERE?" and pointed to the words, "YOU WILL." Almost 44 percent of people who saw the ad clicked on it.

Advertisers were quick to pay attention to the internet, thanks in large part to the explosion in personal computer sales. In 1994 there were sixteen million people online. Two years later there were seventy million people connected to the World Wide Web. I graduated high school in 1996 and recall having access to the internet at school, but at home we had a word processor with no connectivity. I remember writing a research paper for my senior year on a screen with green lettering. Once I finished the paper, I printed it on a DOS printer. By the time I got on the college campus in the fall of 1996, I was using Microsoft Word on a PC and printing on a laser printer.

The early days of digital marketing were all about click bait and campaigns to get users to click on their ads. Advertisers today have to be more creative to get people's attention. Ask me to click on something today and the first thought that goes through my mind is that this is spam or a virus.

As more and more Americans got online, they also signed up for email addresses. Emails were the first big form of digital marketing and still used with success today. There really is nothing new under the sun. Businesses used to spend thousands of dollars on catalogs they would mail to your house every year. As a boy, I loved it when the Sears Christmas catalog would arrive. I would get my pen out and circle every toy I wanted. Now as an adult, I save emails with coupons on products I need.

We take for granted how easy it is to order what we need, but Amazon launched in 1994, eBay debuted in 1995, and soon the world of digital marketing would change when Google launched in 1998.

By the year 2000 there were 361 million internet users. Ten years later that number was 1.97 billion. Creating websites became easier for companies with the invention of website templates, like WordPress. The dot-com boom was on, and every TV, radio, and billboard ad pointed us to a website.

In 2003, the BlackBerry smartphone was introduced in the market. Apple released their first iPhone in 2007. That meant the internet was no longer just an in-home or at the office experience. Now people can take the internet with them whenever and wherever.

Social media started to get on people's radar around 2006-2007, but the 2010s were all about the growth of Facebook, LinkedIn, and other well-known platforms. Advertisers started to create more personal ads to push out on social media. This led to influencer marketing, which uses people with a large social media following to promote products.

The global digital ad spending is expected to reach $441 billion in 2022, an increase of 13.3 percent over the previous year, and experts say by 2024 that number will exceed half a trillion to $524 billion. That is an 85.7 percent increase from 2018.

Forty-six percent of the total global ad spend is now on digital marketing, according to an article published in WebStrategies Inc. in 2020.

Online video and mobile were reportedly the most popular digital marketing channels in 2021. More than 90 percent of marketers invested in these areas. To put that into perspective, the same study showed seven out of ten advertisers had a bigger budget for online video with only three percent spending less. Sixty-four percent spent more on mobile, noting that consumers are spending four out of every five digital minutes on mobile devices versus other devices.

It is impossible to get your mind fully around the growth of digital marketing. In fact, these numbers are estimated, and the actual growth could far exceed any expectation. The reality is, if you own a business, you need a digital marketing strategy.

Email Marketing

WE DISCUSSED EMAIL campaigns in Chapter Two when we looked at the different forms of written media, but email campaigns are also part of digital marketing.

You might be asking, do email campaigns still work? According to a report released by Hubspot, email generates $42 for every $1 spent. Talk about an amazing ROI. There are more than four billion email users today and 78 percent of marketers report an increase in email engagement in recent years.

Like all marketing campaigns, the answer for if you should consider emails starts with your target demographic. Are you trying to reach Boomers? The same study showed that 74 percent of Baby Boomers think email is the most personal outlet to communicate with brands. The younger generations don't ignore emails, they just respond to emails differently. A survey released by Adobe in 2018 found that young people preferred emails over text messages and chats. The reason given was they valued work-life balance and found emails to be non-urgent and not disruptive.

If you have never created an email campaign, where do you get started? First you need to collect email addresses from your customers and potential customers. You can purchase email lists from a third-party. Most of those lists have been sold to hundreds of companies and spamming prospects may not be the best use of your marketing dollars. Most email servers will start to move unread emails into the spam or junk folder.

Is it illegal to send a spam email in the United States? No, it is actually legal to send spam emails in the United States, though this is not the case in every country. But is it wise? I don't think it is a good idea to send unsolicited emails. I recommend you send emails to people who have opted in to receive them. Give people a reason to want to get your emails.

If you are going to buy a list and send spam emails, there are some laws you need to be aware of to avoid paying penalties up to $16,000.

First, make sure you don't have any misleading information in the header of your email. Deceptive or misleading subject lines are also illegal. You can't make your email seem like a personal message, when in fact it is an advertisement. To that end, you need to identify your message as an advertisement. You need to include the physical mailing address of your business. You must include an option for recipients to opt out of future emails. Honor the opt outs within ten days of receiving the request. If you use a third-party vendor to send emails, make sure you monitor their process to ensure you are not breaking the law.

Asking customers to sign up for your emails is a better strategy in my opinion. You still need to follow the same guidelines to protect your business, but you are going to see a better return on your investment. If someone likes your business, an email is a nice way to continue to remind them of the products or services you offer.

It does take longer to build an email list this way, so if you are impatient, you can purchase an email list; just make sure you are buying a list that fits your target demographic and be prepared for the ROI to be much lower.

The more successful email campaigns are optimized for mobile devices. Most consumers will see your email on their phone, so test your email blast on a mobile device before sending to your customers.

Get smart with your emails, don't just send one email to every prospect. Send emails based on demographics or previous purchases. If you owned a clothing store that sold both men's and women's fashion, consider who is signing up for the email. Write the script for the appropriate subscriber. An example might be, "Ladies, what are you getting your husband for Father's Day?"

Smart email campaigns will retarget previous purchases. Amazon does a great job of this tactic. We get emails all the time for products that have a shelf life, like vitamins. The email might read, "Your thirty-day supply of Acme Vitamin is about to run out, would you like to order your next bottle now?"

Track your results. I love email campaigns that tie into your CRM (Customer Relation Management) tool. There you can track open rate and response rate. If you set up your Google Analytics you can also track how many people went to your website from your email blasts. If you don't track your results, how do you know if it's working or not?

Think about when you are sending the email. Most companies blast emails overnight, so you might consider a different time of the day to get attention. When is your target demographic most likely to read or respond to your email? You might consider doing some A/B testing until you get the most traction on your emails. If you own a restaurant, sending an email before mealtime makes sense. If I didn't plan for dinner and I get an email with a coupon to one of my favorite restaurants reminding me of how much I love their food, I am more inclined to respond. If the same restaurant emailed me overnight, I might be inclined to ignore the email and forget about it as the day progresses.

Content is king, so take the time to design an email that will get someone's attention and not get lost in the hundreds of other emails they get daily.

There is a lot to think about, and we are just scratching the service of what makes for an effective email campaign. Consider hiring a professional company to at least help you get started.

Influencer Marketing

ENDORSEMENTS ARE NOT a new concept to marketing. Celebrities have been using their name and likeness to sell products for years. What makes influencer marketing different is what defines a person as an influencer. In the world of digital marketing, an influencer is all about the number of social media followers. Some people really are just famous for being famous.

While the older generations might question what a YouTube star would know about selling a product, the same could be said about a TV star. Why do we trust people we don't know? When viewers watch a TV star from the comfort of their living room, it feels personal to them. Each night that person is on TV talking to them, telling stories about their lives. Overtime they feel like they know that person. So, when the celebrity endorses a product, it's like a friend is endorsing it.

The same is true in the world of social media. People build up large followings by just being themselves or doing something that gets attention. Over time their followers trust them and feel like they are a part of their daily lives.

This is an effective way to break through the algorithms of social media. You can boost your post as we discussed in the last chapter, but users will know it is a paid promotion. But if you can pay an influencer to talk about your product on their social feed to their thousands or millions of followers, that could be money well spent.

Not to continue to drive home demographics, but it is key to any marketing plan. Pick influencers that reach your target demo over ones that just have the highest number of followers. Also consider what platform you want to market on before deciding on the influencer you want to approach. Visual products do well on Instagram and YouTube, where business related products perform best on LinkedIn.

Do your homework and then start to search for people that fit your criteria. You don't have to hire a mega-superstar to endorse your company. Micro-influencers who have less than 2,000 followers might be a better fit for your brand and your budget. The price is all over the place, there is no rate card for this type of marketing. But according to Sprout Social, the overall average price in 2017 was $271 per post. Broken down, the micro-influencers charged about $83 a post and the larger influencers with more than 100,000 followers charged about $763 a post.

Some of the savvier influencers have agents. Yes, there are some people who have agents just because of their social media followers. The closest I ever got to an endorsement deal was when Lipton Tea asked me to try a new product and comment about it online. They sent me the tea for free, that was my payment. So, it could be as simple as asking someone to sample and comment on your product.

Set a budget, manage expectations, and track results. So much of marketing comes down to those three things.

Affiliate Marketing

THIS IS POWER in numbers and any time you can find other people to help sell your products or services that is a win. Affiliate marketing is a digital strategy where you pay other individuals or companies a fee to promote your business on their website.

This is like what we referred to as "per inquiry ads" for TV and Radio. Where with influencers you pay a fee per post, here you pay people a fee every time they bring you clients. So you might have offer codes or track where clicks are coming from and pay for the leads.

Search Engine Marketing

SEARCH ENGINE MARKETING (SEM) is a term used to describe the digital marketing strategy of increasing the visibility of a website in the search engine results.

There has been a shift in the meaning of SEM over the years. Originally Search Engine Marketing referred to both organic and paid search advertising. Now your organic searches fall under its own category of Search Engine Optimization (SEO), which we covered in Chapter Seven. Search Engine Marketing now exclusively refers to paid search advertising.

Some marketing agencies might still consider SEO to be a part of SEM, but for practical purposes think of SEO as what you do to help people find your website organically. SEM is when you spend marketing dollars to promote your website.

Why is it important to promote your website? Like any marketing dollars you spend, the idea is to get the word out about your business to prospects or remind current clients of your products or services. How many times do you go past the first page of a Google search? Paid searches help your website get discovered.

Another term for SEM is pay-per-click (PPC). This is a cost-effective way to market your business. You only pay for results. Let's say you own a pet supply store that sells everything from dog food to cat toys. Your competition would be the bigger box stores like PetSmart. If a prospect did a search for a particular brand of bird seed, a PPC campaign would show your website near the top of their search. If they clicked on that ad, you would pay for that result. But if they got distracted, and never clicked on your ad, you would not be charged.

You are also marketing to consumers at the point of sale. When a consumer is searching for a product, it is a good indicator they are ready to make a purchase.

How does SEM or PPC work? You buy keywords. Keywords are the words that people type in to search for a business. In the example above, you might purchase the keyword "bird seed." Once you select the keywords you want to purchase, you then select a geographic location for the ad. This is known as geotargeting. You want to target your local market to drive business to your website and physical store location. Next you will be prompted to create a text-based ad for display in the search results. The final step is to set the maximum price that you are willing to pay per click. Your cost-per-click (CPC) is part of a bidding process that determines where your ad is placed. The highest bidder gets a better placed ad. But your actual CPC may not be the maximum you set. It comes down to a formula that also takes into account your competitor's Ad Rank (their maximum bid multiplied by their Quality Score) and your own Quality Score (your clickthrough rate, relevance of your keywords, quality of your landing page, etc.), which then determines your actual CPC.

Ready to give it a try? Google Ads and Bing Ads are the two biggest players in the SEM market. Under Google Ads you can purchase on the Google Search Network, which gets you displayed on all Google. com searches. You can also buy ads on the Google Display Network, which opens your searches to Google-owned properties like YouTube, Blogger, and Gmail. Bing Ads gets you SEM on Yahoo's search engine and Bing searches.

Google is bigger and will cost you more, but will get you more results. Google.com generates 62 percent of all core search queries in the US. They generate 96 percent of their revenue from SEM, all made one click at a time. Just how big is Google? They control about 75 percent of the search engine share and report 83,787 searches every second of every day. They are so big their company has become a verb. "Can I Google that for you?"

Remarketing and Facebook Pixel

REMARKETING, ALSO KNOWN as retargeting, is a great way to try to capture prospects who went to your website but left before making a purchase. For a variety of reasons, not everyone is ready to make a purchase the first time they visit your website. They could be searching and comparing your company with your competitors, or they could simply get interrupted during the process of checking out on your website.

An example might be when you are shopping for a used car. You know what you want, now you just want to find who has the exact vehicle for the best price. After searching a few sites during your lunch hour, you get distracted with your work. Later you open a website to book a hotel for an upcoming business trip and to the right side of the list of hotels you see an ad for the vehicle you looked at during lunch. That is a remarketing ad that the local car dealership paid for to try to capture your business.

These ads will show up on future searches, other websites, social platforms, and some apps depending on if you purchase via the Google Search Network or Google Display Network. Of course, you can duplicate the campaign and purchase on both networks. I did a Google search for office cubicles in August when we were looking at remodeling a space in our office. Months later and I am still seeing an ad on LinkedIn and a couple of other places for a business that sells cubicles.

It is not a perfect system. Remarketing follows your device, but it also remarkets to other devices on the same internet. Back to my earlier example about if companies are listening to your conversations, if someone in your building searches for a product with remarketing, you might see the ad on your devices. The best example of this was the time I was served an ad on my iPhone to purchase Iowa Hawkeye gear. I am not an Iowa fan, my team is the Baylor Bears, but my VP of Sales was a huge Iowa fan. At some point he no doubt searched for Iowa gear on his phone or laptop. We shared an internet connection at work, and that sports gear site followed my device all the way to my home.

When you set up a campaign, you can choose to remarket using a pixel or a list. A pixel is a short piece of code placed on your website that drops a cookie onto your visitor's web browser. That pixel then tracks the prospect wherever they go online, placing your ad to remarket to them. A list is when you give Google a list of emails to track and target your ads. You have more control over the list, in that you are targeting your specific customers. But the catch is that the emails need to be Google emails.

Google AdWords has some easy-to-follow videos online to help you set up this process. You can get very detailed with what you want to remarket. Like the example with the used car dealership, you make the remarketing campaigns product specific.

Facebook Pixel works the same way, but in this case when a prospect visits your website a cookie is placed on their browser that is specific to Facebook and Instagram ads. It also ties into your Facebook and Instagram apps.

Before you consider purchasing any of these options, study the latest in phone manufactures' push for more privacy. The tracking codes are starting to be blocked by the latest version on Apple devices.

Mobile Marketing

IN 2011, I WAS asked to sell a texting program to non-profits. The text-to-give market was growing but limited. The largest donation that a person could give at the time was $10 and it was billed through their cell phone provider. The product we sold sent a link to a secure credit card gateway that opened the door for donations of any amount.

What I learned in the process was the potential to use texting as a form of marketing. The company I worked with told me of the possibilities that existed ten years ago, that the public was not ready to accept. A business could geo-target cell phone numbers based on cell towers, meaning as soon as a cell phone pinged a particular cell tower, you could send it a text with a coupon for a local restaurant. I haven't seen this kind of detailed use yet, but don't be surprised to see this in the future.

But like emails, text messages are fast becoming a way we interact with companies. Down the street from my office is one of my favorite hamburger restaurants. They offer a check-in service, where every tenth time I check in I get a free burger. Kind of like the old punch card systems, but I have to enter in my cell phone. Brilliant. Now I get text messages from them periodically with specials of the day. The text always arrives just before the lunch hour.

I get text messages from a clothing store where I recently purchased a new sports coat. The messages remind me that I have a coupon for 40 percent off that is about to expire.

My dentist sends me a text message asking me to confirm my upcoming appointment. I am prompted to replay "Confirm" or "Cancel," with a reminder that failure to cancel within twenty-four hours will cost me $50.

There are so many possibilities when it comes to using text messages to market your business. The benefits include a higher open and response rate than email, the ability to drive business faster with coupons and deals of the day, building a loyal following with your customers, the ease to which people can opt in or out of the messages, and it is cost effective.

Pro-tip, check to see if your CRM offers a texting option before researching vendors that provide this service. Any time you can tie your marketing into your CRM it helps you better track results with your customers.

Conclusion

DIGITAL MARKETING IS all the rage right now. Everyone wants to know what to do about their digital marketing strategy. In fact, you might have been tempted to skip the other chapters and go right to Chapter Nine. Don't worry, you are not alone.

You need a digital marketing strategy, but it needs to be a part of your overall marketing plan. Don't sit down and start with your digital strategy until you know how you are going to market your brand in general. Be proactive, not reactive. Don't read this chapter and run out tomorrow and start remarketing your website. We are going to discuss what an overall plan looks like for your business in Chapter Twelve. Be patient, a good marketing plan takes time.

One other footnote: we are going to take a deep dive into content marketing in Chapter Eleven, but it is important to note that whatever form of digital marketing you decide to take on for your business, the content is key. It is not enough to have an email campaign, hire an influencer, start an affiliate program, purchase search engine marketing, remarket on Google, Bing, and Facebook, and send text messages to your customers. You need a content marketing strategy.

10

LISTING YOUR BUSINESS

A FEW YEARS ago, one of our team members heard about a new barbeque restaurant that opened near our office. The rumors were that the food was so good there was a line that spanned outside of the establishment during the lunch hour. We were sold. Barbeque lunch on a Monday, why not?

We went online to confirm the address and hours of operation, and all jumped in one car (this was back when our company was small enough to ride in one vehicle) and we drove to barbeque heaven.

The experience turned out to be a dumpster fire, both in the literal and figurative sense. When we pulled up to the restaurant, we discovered there were no lines; in fact there were no cars in the parking lot at all. What we found instead was a dumpster that had somehow caught on fire next to the business. A couple of employees were out front with a panicked look on their faces and then we heard the sound of the fire trucks pulling up to extinguish the flames. What the heck?

Turns out the new popular restaurant was closed on Mondays. I am not sure why there were employees working that day, and I am still not sure how the dumpster caught on fire. But what I can tell you is we did not eat barbeque that day. We drove away disappointed, and it took us months before we thought about the place again to give them a second try.

What this new business failed to do is not unique to them; I see many small businesses make the same mistake. They did not claim their online presence and therefore did not have the correct hours of operation listed. Had we seen that they were closed on Mondays, we might have planned to visit the next day and it could have become a quick favorite that we visited several times in the months before we, in reality, finally did try the place. Think about the lost business from one easy mistake that could have been corrected for free.

Listing your business online does not take a lot of time, does not cost you any dollars, and can potentially save you from your own dumpster fire. Figuratively, of course. I can't help you with the literal fires.

History of Listing Businesses

ONE OF MY favorite TV shows growing up was *Little House on the Prairie*. Richard Bull played the role of Nells Oleson, the owner of Oleson Mercantile. The general stores were the Walmarts of its day, where locals went to purchase a variety of items. You knew the store hours because they were posted on the front door, or because you frequented the establishment enough to know when they were open. And if you wanted to know what was available for sale, you got on your horse and rode into town. Listing your business in early American history was really that simple.

In larger cities a business might take an ad out in the local newspaper to advertise the store hours and products available. Bigger companies would print large catalogs and mail them to potential customers.

On March 10, 1876, Alexander Graham Bell successfully made the first phone call when he was speaking to his assistant Thomas Watson. "Mr. Watson, come here, I want to see you," were the first words spoken over a telephone line.

Bell cofounded the American Telephone and Telegraph Company in 1885, known today simply as AT&T, after being awarded the first successful patent for telephone technology. Thus, Bell is often credited for being the inventor of the telephone.

The New Haven Telephone Company in Connecticut published the first phone book. It consisted of a list of names of all fifty subscribers. There were no numbers listed, because the early phone companies paid an operator to make the connections for its customers.

As the telephone industry took off, entrepreneur Reuben H. Donnelley saw an opportunity and printed the first classified telephone directory in 1886 in which businesses were able to advertise. As legend has it, three years earlier a printer in Cheyenne, Wyoming ran out of white paper when printing a telephone directory and used yellow paper instead.

It is funny to think about now, but as a kid growing up in the 1980s, we used the Yellow Pages all the time before leaving the house. If my parents needed to hire a repairman, they would look through the phone book. When I was looking for a particular baseball card for my collection, I would look up the phone number of the baseball card store and call to inquire if they had the card. Before I dialed the number, I would check to see when they were open.

Businesses started to game the system, changing their name to start with the letter "A" to get at the top of the listing. Want to know why there are so many companies that start with the letters "ABC?" They were trying to get more business from the phonebook. Before there was search engine optimization and purchasing pay-per-click ads on Google, you had to optimize the name of your business.

I worked my way through college, and for a couple of weeks I had three jobs at the same time. I got paid to deliver phone books in the morning. I worked at the local newspaper in the early evening hours, calling on citizens asking them to subscribe to the paper. Then at night I would walk across the street and host the request-and-dedications shows on the local country radio station. So it was possible that I delivered your phone book, called your house, and you heard me on the radio on the same day. I was an early media mogul.

The internet has changed how people look for businesses. We don't pick up a phone book anymore; I can't even remember the last time a phone book showed up on my doorstep. No, we all pick up our smartphones and check a few sites to get information. And that is why it is so important to make sure you have the proper information listed online.

Listing Your Business is Important

BRIGHTLOCAL PUBLISHES A "Local Consumer Review Survey" annually that shows how prospects search for products and services. According to their findings, 93 percent of consumers use the internet to find a local business.

Of those looking online, 87 percent say they read online reviews for local businesses. That number has dramatically increased in recent years. Only 48 percent of those surveyed said they would visit an establishment with fewer than four stars on their reviews.

Having incorrect information can cost you business. A survey of digital marketing professionals shows that 73 percent of consumers lost trust in local businesses that had incorrect information online, blaming the brand and not the listing service.

The same survey showed that 71 percent of people will go online to confirm an address for a business before visiting the location for the first time. If you have the wrong address, 67 percent will lose trust in your brand.

Let's face it, the first impression of your business is your online presence. I am surprised how many local businesses I talk to that have never thought to make sure their online listings were correct. In fact, I run across several small business owners who have never taken the time to claim their online listings. If this is you, I have some great news: this is not hard, it does not take a lot of your time, and will result in helping you increase your customer base, leading to more sales.

Allow me to drive home the importance of listing your business properly. You can spend a lot of good money on marketing efforts and see little to no results because your online listings are wrong or nonexistent. Survey after survey shows that when a prospect sees your ad on TV, hears your ad on radio, reads your print ad in the local newspaper, or even sees your ad online, they will still search for your business.

Imagine if you owned a local bakery and you decided to spend some marketing dollars on radio, TV, and the local newspaper. Most people will catch your marketing efforts in a passive way, meaning they are multitasking. They are hearing your messaging, but at the same time they are engaged in other activities. Listening to your radio ad as they pay attention to the traffic around them. Having a conversation with a family member as your TV commercial airs. Or perhaps they are eating breakfast as your digital ad in the online version of the local newspaper is on the side of the sports article they are reading.

With frequency and consistency, your marketing efforts will lead to more sales, but not having the proper listing could be benefiting your competitors. Imagine spending money on marketing that helps your competition. It happens. Using the bakery example, say a prospect decided to treat their office to an afternoon sweet. They remember your commercial but can't recall the exact name of your establishment. So they search on Google Maps for local bakeries. Your competition has taken the time to update their information and show up on Google. But your business is not listed. Who gets the business from your marketing dollars? Even if they remember your business name, if they can't locate it on Google Maps, they are not likely to visit your bakery.

Did you know it's possible that your business is already listed online, and you don't even know it? As people visit different stores and tag a business, Google will create a location. This allows others to check in at that location and even start to leave reviews or comments about the business. All while the owner has no idea people are tagging and commenting on their business. Studies show that 56 percent of small businesses are unclaimed on Google.

Unclaimed businesses often lead to the wrong information being posted, like the wrong office hours. In the world of online reviews, it is always good practice to respond publicly and try to correct any legitimate issues. More on that in a moment.

The worse case scenario is having a competitor or a prankster claim your business online, giving them direct access to current and potential customers. This could destroy your reputation and potentially your business.

But it's not just Google, you need to make sure your business is properly listed on all the listing services, including social media.

Google My Business

THE FIRST STEP to gaining control of how your business is listed is to set up a free Google My Business account. This will help you update information listed on Google searches and Google Maps. Remember Google dominates the search engine market, so you want to make sure your information is current with Google. Go to google.com/business to get started. You will need a Gmail account. I suggest you set up a new Gmail that is tied to your business and not use a personal Gmail.

Once you are logged into your account you can add or claim your business. You can start to update your information, but you need to verify you are the owner or manager of the business to properly update information and get informed when others leave reviews. Google will send you a letter in the mail with a code that allows you to verify your account.

The information you can update includes a primary category and additional categories. The categories help Google know what product or service you offer to help people find you. In the case of Centerpost Media, we list our primary category as Marketing Agency, but we also have additional categories listed as media company, media consultant, television station, marketing consultant, video production service and internet marketing service, to name a few. If someone searches for video production in our local area, they will find Centerpost Media listed as an option. The idea is to list all the categories in which you offer a product or service. You must select from categories available by Google; you can't make up new categories.

You want to make sure your address is correct. You can also add your service areas. The service areas let Google know where you do business or where your customers are coming from. If you are in the service business, like a plumber or electrician, this is where you list what areas you are willing to send your crew. I live in the big metroplex of Dallas-Fort Worth, so a plumber in Dallas might not call on homes in Fort Worth. In our case we list the entire DMA because we have Account Executives who live on both sides of the metroplex. If you do not have a physical location, you can still set up a Google My Business Account and click on the option to not include an address. Your business will not show up in Google Maps but can still be searched on Google.

If you own a restaurant or bar, you can upload your menu. These options show up when you select certain categories. There is even a way you can include an option to book a reservation or place an order.

Check to make sure your hours of operation are correct and make a note to update the hours as they change. This could include seasonal changes; perhaps you are open later during the holiday shopping season. But it can also include noting the days your office is closed. You can pre schedule days you are going to be closed. As an example, our company is closed on Thanksgiving Day and the Friday after Thanksgiving every year. So we update our hours to reflect that our office is closed on those days. Remember my barbeque restaurant example? Avoid frustrating prospects by letting them know your office hours.

The pandemic drove this point home for a lot of small businesses. More people relied on online searches to check if an establishment was open during the national lockdown. Google also added Covid-19 related protocols to help customers know if the business was taking extra precautions to keep their customers safe. We added information to let our clients know that face coverings were required during the height of the pandemic. But as the laws relaxed in Texas, we updated our information that face coverings had become optional. This is a special case to highlight, but something to keep in mind. As conditions change, Google will add features to help you communicate to your prospects and current customers.

You can also list the products you sell or the services you offer. Again, all this information is to help prospects find you when they are searching online for what you have to offer.

Make sure you include your company's profile description. You want this description to match the branding you have on your website and social media. Small businesses will update and tweak their messaging early on until they find what works for them, so make sure this is updated and current.

Add photos of your store front and images of the inside of your office. This helps prospects know what to look for when pulling up to your business for the first time. We own a cool retro 1950s storefront building in downtown Arlington, Texas, that is our corporate headquarters. If you didn't know what to look for, you might miss our office. Photos also help your profile stand out from your competitors.

You can add posts to your Google account. Use this option to promote specials or new products and services you offer.

Google gives you insights into how people are searching for your business and what action items they take after finding you. If they go to your website, search for directions, or call your business, you can see those data points.

Google is crowdsourced, meaning they allow the public to add photos and suggest changes to your information. But when you own the business through Google My Business, you get to approve or reject the suggested changes. I find our clients are very helpful in our process, adding new service areas and suggested services we have offered them.

Finally, the best part is the Google reviews. You will receive emails every time someone leaves you a review, giving you the opportunity to respond to the reviews through your Google My Business account. You want to respond to all reviews in a timely manner, even if it's just a quick note of thanks. Pay really close attention to the negative reviews you might get. As I mentioned earlier, you also want to respond to the negative reviews to see if you can turn a disgruntled customer into a happy customer. Some people just like to complain, and the general public can pick up on the difference between a legitimate complaint and someone who is just seeking attention. I still recommend you respond in kind to the attention seekers at least once.

Want more reviews? You have to be careful not to run a campaign or offer incentives to get positive reviews. Just like people can tell when someone just wants attention, if all the reviews look like an employee wrote them or they were prompted, it can backfire. But it is okay to ask for reviews from clients. We post QR codes in our office to give our clients an easy way to post a review. We don't give them a script or pressure anyone to review our company, we simply give them the option if they are interested.

As a CEO, I love it when clients will give a positive review that mentions one of our team members. I will make it a point to publicly praise that employee for going the extra mile to make a client feel welcomed.

There are other options when you sign up for a Google My Business Account, including creating a marketing ad to promote your business. But even if you never spend a penny on marketing with Google, take the time to set up this account and own and manage how your business is displayed online.

Yelp

I ALWAYS RECOMMEND businesses start with setting up a Google My Business account because that will notify other listing services like Yelp.

Yelp is up there with Google when it comes to how people search and look for businesses. The latest available data shows that there are 178 million unique monthly visitors to Yelp. Customer reviews data indicates that 97 percent of Yelp users will make a purchase after visiting the app.

Like Google My Business, the first thing you want to do is claim your business on Yelp. Once claimed you can login to biz.yelp.com to update your information.

You will find the same information needs to be updated, like the location of your business and hours of operation. You can also add the services you offer with main and subcategories.

There are some differences; the most noticeable are the upcharges from Yelp versus Google. If you want to display your logo on Yelp, it will cost $1 a day. You can purchase what Yelp calls highlights, to show prospects things like how many years you have been in business or if you are women owned and operated. The highlights will cost you $2 a day.

Yelp is also more selective on reviews that are displayed. If multiple reviews come in around the same period, Yelp will not display those reviews even if they are legitimate customers leaving a comment.

Depending on your business, you might consider setting aside a portion of your marketing budget for the add-ons. Yelp is very popular on restaurant and nightlife searches. People looking for a place to eat will go to Yelp to find options, read reviews, look at menus, and even book a table through the app.

Facebook

WE COVERED SOCIAL media in detail in Chapter Eight, but it is worth noting that Facebook is the second most searched website for information. Make sure your hours of operation and business details are current on your Facebook business page. Track the reviews and comments and respond in a timely manner. You can do this all from your Facebook for Business page or app.

Other Listing Options

GOOGLE, YELP, AND Facebook are the top sources people go to find information about local businesses. But there are several other listing sites you need to consider updating. There are more than seventy different sites people can search to find your business' information.

Some of the more popular ones to consider include: Angie's List, Better Business Bureau, Bing, LinkedIn, Manta, TripAdvisor, Thumbtack, Yellow Pages Director Inc., and YP.com.

This can be overwhelming for a small business owner. The good news is there are options available for you to update your information once, and have it auto-populate most of the listing services. I recommend you reach out to a digital marketing agency for help to save you some time.

Conclusion

YOU WANT PEOPLE to be able to find your business, so making sure your company is properly listed makes sense. Adding the products and services you offer helps prospects know you're an option that is available.

Reviews are an important part of the consumer buying process today, so you want to seek reviews from your clients and respond to reviews online in a timely manner.

Having your business listed wherever possible comes down to Search Engine Optimization (SEO). The more places you're listed with correct and credible information, the more likely consumers are to find you when doing an online search.

11

CONTENT MARKETING

IN 2007 MY wife and I purchased a home in the Atlanta area. My job had moved us from Fort Worth, Texas, and we were excited to start our new life in Georgia. We closed on our home on October 30th that year and our furniture arrived on Halloween. In hindsight that might have been an omen of things to come.

Wanting our three-year-old to feel at home in our new neighborhood, my wife purchased a costume and took her down the street trick-or-treating. I stayed behind and started unpacking boxes and passed out candy at the front door. There were so many kids that it got to the point that I decided to turn off my front porch light and focus on getting some boxes unpacked. Turning off your front porch light is the international symbol for "we are out of candy." No sooner did I turn off the light did I see a kid running toward our front door. I saw him raise his arm and throw something toward the house and heard something hit the threshold of the door. We got egged. Welcome to the neighborhood. As I was cleaning off the eggs another neighbor came over with a fresh baked pie to welcome us. She had seen the moving van. What a day.

What we could not predict at the time was that the company that purchased the networks I worked for would only keep them for eighteen months before selling them off to a group of investors who lived in Texas. Had we known our stay in the peach state would be less than two years, we would have rented and not purchased a home.

In 2008, the housing bubble broke, causing a major housing crisis. We had been living in our new home for less than six months and we were already upside down on our mortgage. When my job was coming to an end in the fall of 2009, I had one offer on the table to work for the new investors and a second offer in the works with a radio station also located in Texas. We had not lived long enough in Georgia to establish connections to find work, so the writing was on the wall that we needed to move back home.

I put the for-sale sign in the yard and moved my family in with my wife's parents as we waited to sell our home. We had one offer come in for less than we owed on the mortgage. We had no other choice but to rent out our home. Renting a home from five states away is not a good idea. But that is for another book. Let's just say our renters were not interested in keeping the property value up.

We moved into a rental home in Arlington, Texas, and tried to make things work. My mortgage payment on our Georgia home was more than I could get in rent. That meant that I was paying for rent on a house in Texas, collecting rent on a home in Georgia, and having to pay more money to the mortgage company in addition to the rent I collected.

All of that led to us short selling our Georgia home in 2010. A short sell is when you sell your home for less than you owe, and your mortgage company forgives the rest of the debt. Normally you are taxed for the difference as income, but the Obama administration pushed for forgiveness of the taxable income. I remember calling the mortgage company to start the process and the lady I talked to was surprised. We had never missed a payment and most people don't ask for a short sale until they have missed payments and are trying to avoid legal issues. People asked me if I was sad to sell our home and not make a profit.

My response was that I was happy to get the nearly $200,000 of debt off my account.

There was one caveat to our short sell. We were prohibited from purchasing another home for a period of time, meaning we would not qualify for funding. We lived in our rental house for six years until we could finally get the funding we needed to purchase a new home.

We liked our rental house, and watched our girls grow from our oldest just starting elementary to going into junior high. Our youngest, who was born in Georgia, remembers the rental house as her first home. But there is just something about owning your own home that is special. We get to decide what color to paint the walls. And we know with each payment we are investing in our future. One day we will sell our home and use the profit for retirement or helping our kids and future grandkids.

There are so many more benefits to owning a home versus renting a home, but what does this have to do with content marketing? I am glad you asked.

Advertising is renting someone else's audience. Content marketing is owning the audience. And like homeownership, there are so many benefits to owning the audience versus renting the audience.

History of Content Marketing

THE CONCEPT OF content marketing is not new, but the term was first used in 1996 by John F. Oppedahl at a journalism conference.

The Content Marketing Institute did a deep dive into the origin of when content marketing was first used. The earliest example found dates back to 1732 when Benjamin Franklin published the first *Poor Richard's Almanack* that was used to promote his printing business.

There have been other famous examples of content marketing. Johnson & Johnson launched the *Modern Methods of Antiseptic Wound Treatment* publication in 1888 that targeted doctors who used bandages. John Deere started the magazine *The Furrow* in 1895, providing information for farmers and selling tractors. *The Furrow* is still in production today.

One of my favorite examples of content marketing is *The Michelin Guide*, launched in 1900. The Michelin Tire Company wanted to increase sales of tires, so they encouraged people to get out and drive and explore new places. More miles on the tires equals more sales of new tires. Even today when you hear of a restaurant earning a Michelin Star, know that that is content marketing. To think celebrity chefs take pride in stars awarded from a tire manufacturer.

In 1904, Jell-O added more than a million dollars in sales by releasing free copies of a recipe book. Of course, the recipes called for more Jell-O.

There are also modern examples of companies using content marketing today. I have already noted that Hallmark and Disney have both used content creation to drive their respective brands. Another great example is Red Bull, the energy drink. Red Bull Media House produces more than 1,200 culture and sporting events a year, according to their website. The content is entertaining but targets the demographic most likely to purchase an energy drink.

And that is the point of content marketing. Creating content to build a following of people most interested in purchasing your product or service.

Pushing Out Content

WHILE THE CONCEPT of content marketing is not new, the avenues available to push out the content are changing.

This book you are reading is a form of content marketing. I am the CEO of a content marketing agency. The biggest hurdle we have in our sales process is education. Once a business owner understands the power of content marketing, they want to do business with us. So why not write a book about how to use media? You could do the same in your industry. What are you an expert at and how can you use that knowledge to help others? That is one of the biggest keys to content marketing, which we will unpack in a moment.

Writing a book is a huge undertaking, even if you enjoy writing. Other options for written content marketing include a weekly article written in your local newspaper, or your company could start a monthly newsletter to give your customers information that adds value. Or if you own a larger business, you can take the newsletter to the next level and publish a quarterly magazine. Email blasts are another form of content marketing. The most affordable option is to start a weekly blog that you publish on your website. Use social media and email to promote your blog. This has the added benefit of providing fresh content on your website to increase SEO.

If writing is not your gift, survey your staff to see if someone has a passion for writing. Hire a ghost writer or freelance writers to help generate content. Or you can hire a content marketing agency to help you come up with strategies of what to write.

You can also use your voice to create content. Podcasting is a growing trend among business leaders. This can not only help you build a loyal following of prospects and current customers, but you can use your podcast to close business. Invite that person you have been courting to be a guest on your podcast. Pro-tip, prospects will give you their personal contact information, like their cell phone number, when invited to be a guest on a show. This is true for all forms of broadcasting, like a podcast, radio show or TV appearance. Connecting with a prospect on a show warms them up for a conversation off-air. It's how most of my program clients use their shows to make money.

If you want to use audio content to get direct results, launch a radio show. Direct results are when someone listens to a radio station, hears your content, and decides to do business with you. Indirect results are when you take that content and post it online and on social media and get more sales from current followers or from prospects not directly tied to the radio station you are broadcasting on. Podcasting is a great start to audio content, but to find prospects you have to spend some dollars to promote your podcast. Podcasting is not a field of dreams that if you start a podcast the listeners will find you. In truth, this is the case with all forms of content you create, but especially true when posting content online only. But a radio show will find prospects who listen to the radio station and catch your show.

Video is powerful and drives SEO. Start by posting videos on your website that help visitors understand your products or services. Keep your videos fresh. You can also post videos on social media and platforms like YouTube. When I need to fix something around the house, the first thing I do is watch a YouTube video. The goal of content marketing is to own your audience. Push out videos that build a loyal following of people interested in what you have to say.

Same with audio, if you are wanting to take your content to the next level you need to broadcast it on TV. Anyone can create a video and push it out to YouTube, but when you are on TV it gives the perception that you are the expert on the topic. You can host a local TV show in your market and center the content around topics related to your business.

If all this seems overwhelming to you, start small and hire a public relations agency to help get appearances on other people's podcasts, radio shows, or TV shows. Use the interview as content you can push out online and on social media. This is what I like to refer to as third-party validation. When you can have a professional personality interview you about your business, that validates your expertise.

That is one of the first things we do with our clients. We book them as guests on one of our local or national TV shows. The client will fill out a guest form to give our hosts an idea of the topics they want to cover. On production day our show host puts our clients at ease and has a one-on-one conversation about their business. We air the interview on TV or radio and the client walks away with content that gives them both direct and indirect results. This is a very affordable entry point into content marketing.

I have noticed a cycle with our clients. They usually start as guests on one of our shows and they quickly get addicted to the power of the media. Mass media helps them tell their story to thousands of people at one time. And there is something exciting about sitting down behind a microphone or in front of a camera.

I recently had the privilege of giving a tour of our corporate offices and studios to a group of students from my alma mater, Howard Payne University. The tour ended with us interviewing four students for five minutes. They all loved the experience and one of the students we interviewed said her heart was racing afterwards. She had competed in Miss Texas and said being interviewed on TV was like being on stage. She was pumped.

Once a client has a few interviews under their belt, they start to explore other ways to create content. For some that means starting a podcast. Others we have helped start their own TV show.

Like YouTube, you can also push content out in the new OTT space; creating shows that air on streaming devices like Apple TV, Roku, and Amazon Fire. There are low entry points to some of these platforms.

Social Media is all about content marketing. You can use these platforms to post videos, excerpts of your blog, and as of the writing of this book, Facebook is exploring options where you can push out your podcasts.

What Makes Good Content

THERE WILL NO doubt be future avenues to push out content not even in the marketplace, but regardless of where you push out content it needs to be good.

This is where most small businesses stop themselves from even trying to create content to market their companies. Who wants to associate their brand with something not good? But there are a few tips to follow to make sure you are creating good content.

Play to your strength. Don't try to be someone or something you are not. Are you a good writer? Do you have good communication skills? Can you tell your company's story in a way that is easy to understand and follow? Are you good at education or is humor your strength?

In truth, most small business owners are not great at creating content without some help. But that is the point of this book, to help you! It's okay to not be a great marketer; chances are you did not go to college to learn marketing. Most small business owners are not marketers. Know when to hire some professional help.

I often tell myself that I can fix anything with the right information and the right tools. I have replaced a broken rearview mirror and cruise control switch on a vehicle. My wife and I have replaced an ignition switch and sunroof motor on our daughter's car. Impressive, right? But there comes a point when the job is too much for me to handle and I hire a mechanic.

The same is true for content marketing. There are some things you can do on your own with the right tools and right instructions. But there also comes a point when you need to hire a professional.

You can write your own content. If you have a computer, you have the right tool. As for instructions, here are some tips to follow.

1. Write about what you know. Choose topics that come natural to you.

2. Keep your content short for blogs, between 500 to 700 words. Too long and you will lose people's attention online. Newsletters or articles can be longer, about 1,500 to 2,000 words. If you are writing a book a good target is around 5,000 words a chapter.

3. Use images to drive home the material for online blogs or newsletters, but make sure you have the copyright. You can take your own pictures or use a service where you can purchase royalty free pictures. I like Pond5. You can go to www.pond5.com for details.

4. Have at least one other person proofread your work. You may be the best writer and perfect at grammar, but you will miss something in your writing. The brain is an amazing organ that

thinks faster than you can type and will often fill in missing words when you read back your material.

5. Offer something of value to the reader. Practical tips, humor, or information on your products are examples. You want the reader to desire to come back for more content.

6. Be personal if the writing has your name on it. People want to get to know you. If you are writing for the company without your byline, find the voice of your organization and write with a consistent style.

7. Be consistent in how often you post your blog, publish your newsletter, or write an article. This is how you build followers who want to read your content. I recommend posting blogs once a week, newsletters monthly, and magazines quarterly. Newspaper columns are typically weekly.

8. Promote this writing on social media, through email, and on your website. This helps prospects find your content.

9. Know when to hire a professional writer. If the process is frustrating to you, or you find you don't have the time to keep up with the demands, hire someone to write on your behalf.

Recording audio is as easy as picking up your smartphone, but I recommend you invest in some additional equipment if this is the direction you want to go. You can purchase a microphone with a USB connection for your laptop. There are recording tools like Audacity that are free that you can download and tweak your audio. Those are the tools, here are the tips.

1. Talk about what you know. Just like writing, you want to touch on subjects that come natural to you.

2. Talk to one person. Audio is very personal; most people listen to a podcast on their commute to work or back home alone. Pretend you are having a conversation with one person if you are the only one on the show. If you have a guest, make the listener feel like they are eavesdropping on your conversation.

3. Use current events to draw in the listener. This is particularly true with radio shows. Look at the headlines and see if you can make a connection to your topic. People follow the news and can more easily follow your train of thought if you pick up on a topic they are already thinking about. Steer clear of hot topic issues that only divide your potential customers.

4. Find a hosting platform that will help you manage your metadata and push your content out to all the major podcasting platforms.

5. Make sure you enter all the proper metadata. This is information related to your content that can be searched online.

6. Tag the people you are interviewing to grow the reach of your content. When you push it out online and tag your guest, that is how you can promote your content on their platforms.

7. Know when to hire a professional. Companies like Centerpost Media can handle all of the production, distribution, and metadata so you can focus just on the content.

You can record some videos from a smartphone and post them online. You have the tool; most phones have HD or higher quality cameras now. As for the right instructions, here are some basic tips for creating a video.

1. Know what you are going to say before you start recording. You need the video to be two minutes or shorter, so be prepared for what you want to discuss.

2. Look at the camera if you are talking to the viewer. It is tempting to look at yourself if you are using a smartphone, but to give the appearance you are making eye contact look directly at the camera lens.

3. You can script your video, but I recommend you just be yourself. It takes a lot of practice to read a script and sound natural, so try just writing bullet points instead to keep your video on track.

4. Don't be afraid to shoot the video a few times to get the desired effect.

5. Edit the video to add in lower thirds and images or other videos to make your content more watchable. There are free tools that help you edit video. If you own a Mac, iMovie is user friendly with built-in tools. If you are on a PC you can use Windows Video Editor or any other compatible software.

6. Lighting. You need to make sure your video is properly lit. If people cannot see you or what you are trying to show, they will not watch your videos. You can use desk lamps, just make sure the lighting is behind the camera. Shooting toward a lamp or the sun will wash out the video, create too many shadows, and make it difficult to see the images.

7. Audio. We need to be able to understand what you are saying. In the world of smartphones, lower resolution video can be forgiven more than bad audio. So make sure you have clean, easy to understand audio.

8. Dress in solid colors. Patterns can give a dizzy effect, so we always recommend you wear solid dark colors when appearing on video.

9. Keep your videos fresh. It's not enough to create and push out videos, you need to push out videos on a consistent basis. This does not have to be weekly, but don't wait months to create your next video.

10. Know when to hire someone to help with your video. There are companies that will come to your office or have a studio you can rent by the hour. We have several clients who come into our studios every so many months to record a fresh video.

Types of Content

THERE ARE TWO basic forms of content marketing. Informative and entertainment. Most small businesses will find it easier to create informative content, but few venture out and create entertaining content.

Let's discuss the entertaining content first to get your mind around what this looks like. When you think about Disney and Hallmark, those are examples of entertainment content marketing. Disney has long promoted their theme parks, movies, and merchandise through the creation of entertainment. Just last year they released a new movie *Jungle Cruise*, based on the popular theme park attraction of the same name. Hallmark has invested a lot of money into making Christmas movies because they want you thinking about Hallmark around the holidays.

Writing a script and producing a movie or made-for-TV drama and comedy is expensive and very hard to pull off. But you could create a reality TV show on a budget that is entertaining. The Gold & Silver Pawn Shop is located on the outskirts of Las Vegas. If you stop by you will recognize the family that owns and operates the store from the hit TV show *Pawn Stars* that aired on the History Channel and is now in syndication.

Editing is the key for reality TV shows. Newsflash, they really aren't that real. To film people working all day in a pawn store would make for boring television. Just watch an episode of *Big Brother After Dark* as an example.

Entertainment content marking also takes a lot of time to produce. I watched an interview where Chip Gaines admitted his frustration with trying to keep up with the demands of recording the number-one cable TV show *Fixer Upper* for HGTV while also trying to raise a family and run a business.

An entertainment podcast is an easier and more affordable option. You can host a roundtable discussion of a topic that draws in your target demographic and use that content to promote your business.

Informative content is where you give free advice related to the products or services you offer. That is the key to content marketing: offering something of value. If all you do is talk about your business and how great you are, you are just producing what we in the business call an infomercial. Infomercials are just longform commercials selling a product. They work, but that is not content marketing.

You want to follow the 80/20 rule and have 80 percent of your content give free advice, tips, and information that can help someone. Then you can use the other 20 percent to remind your followers that you can help them with their needs. This book is a perfect example; if you read this book and follow the tips you will be successful. But I also remind you that our company can help you with all these services.

When my wife started her cookie business, she followed a woman online who created videos that showed some tips on how to decorate cookies more easily; practical tips that helped her perfect her craft for her new business. The same woman also sold cookie cutters in all shapes and sizes to make the perfect cookie. She knew her target demo was ladies who were looking to make an extra passive income, so she created informative content to market her company.

When we wanted to eat healthier, my wife found a woman online who created a brand called Skinnytaste. She pushed out content every week in the form of menus she created for her followers. You can download the menu and go to her website to learn how to cook each recipe. You can also purchase the food to be delivered to your home. Great tips and information for her followers to market Skinnytaste.

To be informative does not mean you have to talk only about your product. When you look at these examples you see one person giving cookie decorating ideas and another pushing out free recipes. They are not creating content that just talks about how their product or service works.

I host a weekly show called *Create. Build. Manage.* that airs on BizTV, BizTalkRadio, and is pushed out on all the major podcasting platforms. I do not use this show to talk about content marketing every week. In fact most weeks we are addressing issues that are important to business owners and entrepreneurs. As I write this chapter in October of 2021, some of the topics we cover include the Great Resignation, supply demand issues, and what to do today to prepare for the new year. The show is based on the three stages of starting a business. You create an idea, build your business, and then manage your business. I use the content to build followers for our company that we can then push out our marketing services.

Content Marketing is the Future

THERE IS MORE content available today than ever before, so why invest in producing more content? It's about spending your marketing dollars wisely. It's about owning your audience. People will follow things they are interested in following. Creating content that is pushed out online, on social media, on radio and TV, and OTT platforms is a long-term strategy. It takes time to build the kind of following that will elevate your company to the next level, but once you get that kind of following it is priceless.

The numbers tell the truth. Seventy percent of marketers are actively investing in content marketing according to a 2019 HubSpot survey. How do marketers measure success? Overall sales are up. Nearly 40 percent of marketers say content marketing is a very important part of their overall marketing plan. And "Content Marketing Strategy" is the most searched query related to content marketing.

Social media is the main platform used to push content marketing, with 94 percent of marketers using that outlet. Podcasting continues to grow, with 75 percent of Americans now familiar with the concept. Video has now overtaken blogs as the most used content marketing format. Eighty seven percent of those who have used video on their website report increased web traffic, leading to 80 percent reporting a direct link between videos and increased sales.

Globally, the content market is set to grow by $418 billion by the year 2025. This is fueled by a huge increase in spending in recent years. A 2019 study released by the Content Council and the Association of National Advertising showed a 73 percent average budget increase over a two-year period in content marketing. The same report projects a 42 percent spending hike by 2022.

This data just highlights the importance of having a content marketing strategy for your business. But before you can have a content marketing strategy, you need a marketing plan, which we will discuss in the next chapter.

Conclusion

YOU DO NOT have to spend thousands of dollars to start marketing your business, but you do need to spend some money. There are free tools available to you, like social media, but having the right tools is not enough. You need to know how to use those tools to effectively market your brand.

We call our company Centerpost Media. At the center of every business is its story, and without the story your business will come crashing down. Think of that image of the center post of a large circus tent. When the circus is done and ready to move to the next town, the elephant is called over to pull down the center post and everyone watches as the tent falls. In business, you are either telling your story or someone else is telling your story and there is a chance they may call over the elephant. You want to control your story. That is what marketing is all about: controlling the story of your business.

Content marketing is a great way for small businesses to tell their story. What makes your business unique from your competitors? What do you offer that is different, needed or wanted? Is it your product? Your customer service? Why would someone want to do business with you?

In truth, you are the expert already. You don't need a blog, video, or podcast to prove it, these platforms just showcase your talents. I love watching the small business owners who come into one of our studios across the country for an interview. Seeing them get excited about what they are passionate about is fun. We don't coach our guests on what to say, we simply ask them about their business. Why did they start their company? What gets them out of bed every morning and ready to get to work?

Taking those passions and creating content is what will fuel future growth. We know the saying that people do business with people, not companies.

But remember, give people a reason to follow you. Don't just promote yourself. Offer free practical advice, tips, information, or entertainment. Finally, be patient and know it takes time to build your following, but once you do you will have customers who will share your content with their own followers. And that is the power of content marketing.

12

WHAT'S BEST FOR YOU?

I HAVE HAD the pleasure of meeting so many interesting entrepreneurs and small business owners over the years. I could honestly write another book about their stories. I love how creative people are when it comes to finding a way to generate income.

We once had a gentleman in our Dallas studio who has made a living training and maintaining pigeons. He owns more than 200 of these birds used for weddings and other special occasions. You can hire him to show up and release the pigeons on cue. When our host asked him how many pigeons he had lost over the years, his response was maybe two.

Then there was the woman who built a nest egg for her family selling cowbells. She got the idea when the Winter Olympics were in Salt Lake City. Now she will sell you a cowbell for everything you can imagine. I can still hear her ringing the bells at the end of her interview saying, "You need more cowbells!"

We have interviewed an alligator hunter from his boat in Colorado, a mom-and-pop jelly and jam shop in Georgia, and the home of the world-famous fruit cake in Texas. Each one of these has the same thing in common: they are small businesses who need help marketing their products. What I have learned over the years is that most of our prospects know they need to be doing something, but they just don't know where to begin. That is why I wrote this book, to help small business owners and entrepreneurs take the first step toward growing their business through media.

What is best for you? I can't possibly answer that question without knowing more about your business. But I can give you a roadmap of questions to answer that will get you on the right path. These are questions I would ask you if we were to sit down over a cup of coffee and talk about your business.

Before we dive into the questions, it is important I give you a nugget of truth. You have to spend money to make money. I am sure someone can give me an example where that was not the case, but as a rule of thumb marketing will cost you money. But if done right, the return on your investment will be worth it.

The Roadmap

Where do you want this trip to take you? What are you trying to accomplish? If you are looking at spending money on marketing, what is your end goal? I always start with this question to get you thinking about what it is that you really want to see happen by marketing your company.

I am not talking about a generic answer. Some examples include increased sales, more social media interactions, or increased visits to your website. I get that those are good answers, but that is not why you are wanting to market your company.

You have a goal in mind for your life. A dream for your business. You did not start your company so that you can sell more products. You started your company for a deeper personal reason. Once you discover or rediscover that passion, it makes this road a much smoother ride.

Here are some possible reasons. You may have started your company because of a personal need. I met a lady who described herself as the "scholarship lady." When her kids were getting ready to go to college, she started researching what scholarship money was available. She found out that thousands of dollars go unclaimed every year. She was so good in her research that the college her daughter chose ended up sending money home because of the number of scholarships awarded. Oh, we totally signed up and used her services. But her passion started with helping her family and out of that grew a passion to help other parents struggling to pay for college. For her it is not about the number of clients who are paying her, it's the number of families she can help.

You might have started your company to pay it forward or give back to the community. Our founder Ed Frazier started BizTV to be a mentor to young entrepreneurs. When Ed was young, he had someone take the time to pour into him, and that continued throughout his career. Ed's passion was to provide the resources that small business owners needed to learn and grow their companies. We talk about putting people over profit in our company, which comes from Ed's original vision. It's not about making a ton of money, it's how many businesses can we help.

Perhaps you started your company to provide for your family, and that's okay. Most small businesses are started out of the simple need to pay for food, shelter, and other life essentials. I know for me, my wife and two daughters are my personal motivation. I want them to have everything they could possibly want in life and then some. Because I love my family, I want to spend time with them. One day I hope to retire and travel the world with my wife. Ask me why I want our business to be successful. It's not about making more money. No, it's about what I would do with more money.

You could have personal career goals that drive you to want to be successful. I worked with one person who always wanted to host a radio show. For her it was not about more sales for her business, it was a dream she wanted to accomplish. Being known is a driving factor for some people. But it can also be checking something off your bucket list.

That is what I mean by what you are trying to accomplish. Just wanting to make more sales is good, but that is not a passion. Your passion is to help others, provide for your family, or build a business that is a benefit to your community. And I want you to be able to do all of that and more!

The second path on the roadmap is pulling over and looking at the roads you have already traveled. What has worked and what has not worked? What have you tried to do already and why do you think it did or did not work for you?

I always want to know your experience with marketing to get an idea of your point of view. Most people I have talked to have tried something with little to no success. Unfortunately, there are a lot of marketing companies that are more interested in closing a sale with you than helping you close more sales. If this describes your story, what did you learn from that experience?

Did you try a social media campaign and it failed? How did it fail? Did you not get the social media interactions you were promised? Did your sales not increase? How long did you try the campaign?

You can pretty much substitute the words "social media" with any form of media and ask the same questions. Often campaigns fail because expectations were not managed on the front end, or you were measuring the wrong results. We will unpack what to measure later in this chapter. For now, I want you to write down everything you have tried before and process what did and did not work with your efforts.

Where on the roadmap are you currently located? You have identified where you want to go, your passion. You have looked at where you have been, the good and the bad. Now look at where you are on the map.

Before you can start any marketing campaign you need a baseline. You need to measure where things stand today, so you can track results. Look at your current sales on your profit and loss statement. Make sure you are comparing apples to apples. I recommend you look at the previous year for true comparison. For example, if I am going to run a new campaign in Q1, I want to look at Q1 from the previous year and track sales against that year. Because of the crazy economic times related to the pandemic, you might need to go further back to get an accurate number.

Google Analytics is another great baseline. Study the numbers from your website over the past twelve months. Get a good idea of the number of visitors you have to your site currently, before starting a campaign.

How many followers do you have on your social media? What kind of interactions were you getting over the past twelve months?

What other data points can you track? Inventory? Foot traffic? Phone calls? There are several possibilities. The point is to understand where you are currently before you start to move toward your destination.

Finally, you need to figure out which path you want to take. I love WAZE because I don't have to think about which route to drive on a road trip. If you work with the right kind of marketing agency, they will be your GPS, helping you navigate around potential road hazards.

If you are driving solo, consider some practical tips. You don't have to spend dollars everywhere at the same time. Unless you are running a Fortune 500 company, you don't have the time or the budget to buy TV, Radio, Print, social media, Digital Marketing, and so on all at the same time. You need to choose the platforms that make sense for your business. And that starts with understanding your target demographic.

Word-of-Mouth Marketing

MOST SMALL BUSINESS owners I meet lack a marketing plan. They might budget for marketing but have not taken the time to sit down and draw out a plan to allocate the line item. But I am being kind because most haven't even included marketing in their budget. The most common response I hear from entrepreneurs when I ask about their marketing strategy is to tell me, "Word-of-mouth."

Let's unpack what exactly a word-of-mouth marketing plan is. Saying you have a word-of-mouth marketing strategy and not actually having a strategy is a kind way of saying you don't have a plan.

When people say their marketing plan is word-of-mouth, most simply mean that they get referrals from current customers or clients; that they are happy with the steady stream of clientele they currently have, and they feel like they don't have to spend marketing dollars to attract new business.

I have had small business owners tell me that they don't want any new business, that they have all the business they can handle today. That is great, but for most who tell me they are overwhelmed working eighty hours a week and the thought of adding more business is too much, my counter argument is asking them if they are happy with the hours they are working or if they would like to have more time at home with their families or friends. Of course they want more time away from work. This goes back to the passion, and an increase in business will allow that owner to hire more help and build more margin in their life.

An effective word-of-mouth marketing plan is when your customers or clients follow three steps:

1. They hear about your service or product.
2. They experience your service or product.
3. They tell others about your service or product.

If your client or customer does not feel special, there will be no word-of-mouth marketing. Or worse, you might have a negative word-of-mouth strategy.

You have to have something that is buzz worthy. You must create the buzz and then encourage the buzz. A few years ago, a local hamburger restaurant in Arlington, Texas created buzz by offering "bootleg chicken." The owners created a family meal that included fried chicken and all the fixings. Because they were a hamburger restaurant, they got creative and only offered the meal to patrons who pulled around back and knocked on the back door with a twenty-dollar bill. Someone would open the door, take your $20 without saying a word and return a couple of minutes later with a bag of food. That is a buzz-worthy campaign. I first heard about it when my friends on Facebook started talking about their experience. We had to try it for ourselves, so we packed up the minivan and drove to the back of the restaurant with a twenty-dollar bill.

There are other ways to create an effective word-of-mouth marketing plan. Chick-fil-A wanted to be known as a clean, fast, and friendly fast-food chain. They set out to train their franchise owners to keep every restaurant clean, make the lines move as fast as possible, and make sure every team member went out of their way to be friendly. Chick-fil-A has run several successful advertising campaigns, but never have you seen the tagline "clean, fast, and friendly." Instead, their advertising centered around campaigns like "Eat Mor Chikin," and "We Didn't Invent the Chicken, Just the Chicken Sandwich." But what is Chick-fil-A known for? When the Covid-19 vaccine became available in America, several people joked on social media that all of America would get their shot in one day if Chick-fil-A oversaw the administering of the vaccine. That is an effective word-of-mouth marketing plan.

Coca-Cola has used advertising to fuel their word-of-mouth marketing, asking people to "share a Coke and a smile." They printed names on their twenty-ounce bottles, which led to people taking pictures of themselves with a Coke bottle and sharing it on social media.

As you can see in these examples, word-of-mouth marketing can happen organically and through marketing. But it is usually a combination of both. Chick-fil-A and Coca-Cola both rely on advertising to drive their sales, not just word-of-mouth.

And if you are going to take this route, you need to make sure people can find your website and your location. This goes back to making sure your SEO is up to date on your website and that your business is properly listed on the various platforms people go to find you. So again, saying you have a word-of-mouth marketing strategy and not actually having a strategy is just a polite way of saying you have no plan.

The Marketing Plan

WHEN IT COMES to travel, my wife is a huge planner. She loves to explore new places with our girls and we never leave the house without laying out an itinerary. She has a clear objective to have fun and maximize our time. She has a defined budget and makes decisions based on that budget. She will study the best time to visit certain attractions and schedule out our days to hit all the nearby places together. The woman is impressive and may have missed her calling to be a travel agent. One time we went to Disney with her side of the extended family. There were a total of ten of us and she had Magic Kingdom planned out down to when we needed to be in line for each ride. On a busy June day at Disney, the longest we had to wait in line for any one ride was thirty minutes.

That is the purpose of a marketing plan. To look at the objective you are trying to achieve, use the financial resources you have available, plan out how to maximize your budget and time, and plan to achieve your goals. It is about being proactive and not reactive.

Going back to my vacation example, we have taken trips that were not planned. We booked a week-long cruise and went with the mindset that we will just go with the flow. We had taken weekend cruises before and packed several things into a couple of days. But with the week-long cruise we decided to not plan and just wake up every day and do whatever we felt like. Perhaps that works for your family, but that did not work for us. We spent more time discussing what we wanted to do than doing something. The girls got bored, which I know is a first-world problem, but my point is that lack of a plan created some tension.

Does this describe your business? Have you sat in your office looking at your sales numbers and decided at that moment something needs to be done? Here is the truth: the foundation for success tomorrow is laid today. Planning today will lead to future success. You cannot come up with a marketing plan today and expect results next week. That is not how marketing works. But the good news is that you are on the right path. You picked up this book because you wanted to make a change in your business. So let's get to planning!

There are some things you need to consider before writing your marketing plan. What are the needs of your clients or customers?

Who is your competition and how do you compare? What direction do you want to take your company in? What objectives are you trying to achieve?

Sales is all about meeting a need, so what are the needs of your clients or customers? You need to answer this question first and give yourself room to make the necessary changes to your products or services to meet a need. I know in our company we had to adjust our products because the needs of our clients changed when the pandemic forced them to change how they did business. We shifted our focus away from commercial advertising to storytelling. We saw that there was a huge need for entrepreneurs to tell their story of how they were adjusting and servicing the community. An interview became more important than a thirty-second ad.

How do you compare to your competition? What sets you apart from other companies that provide similar services? I confess I don't spend a lot of time focused on our competition, but there is value in knowing where you stand in the marketplace. I always want Centerpost Media to be the best, so I push my team to focus on what we are good at doing. There are some services we offer that we are not the best at, so we outsource those services, or we have even been known to recommend our competitors. That might seem strange, but it fits our word-of-mouth strategy to put people over profits. Our marketing efforts focus on what we do best, which is content creation.

Know the direction you want to take your company before writing your marketing plan. If your overall plan is to open a new location, that will help you know how to plan your marketing. We have local sales offices in Dallas, Austin, Houston, Los Angeles, and Atlanta. But we have plans to open offices in Phoenix, Pittsburg, Minneapolis, and San Antonio in the new year. Part of our marketing plan is to pre-market to those cities to let prospects know we are coming.

What objectives are you trying to achieve? Beyond just increasing sales, get specific. Is there a certain level of growth you want to see in the new year?

You want to define clear and realistic goals. You cannot be so broad that it is impossible to track or know where to begin. The idea is to plan the best strategy, put that strategy into action and measure results along the way.

Once you understand these principles, you are ready to write out your marketing plan.

The Playbook

IN TEAM SPORTS you need a playbook to succeed. The playbook is a list of offensive or defensive plays that when called put each player in position for success. Part of what makes sports so fun for me to watch is the chess match between coaches, trying to out-call the opponent.

Imagine if a team did not have a playbook. If a coach just told his team to go out there and try to win the game. He never called any plays, just watched his team run around and try to score or stop the other team from scoring. Have you ever watched a peewee league game? That is pretty much what would happen. The players would look confused, be lined up in the wrong place, and no doubt would draw a lot of penalties.

As much as that sounds ridiculous, that is exactly what most small business owners do to their team, their staff. There is no playbook and the employees all run around trying to figure things out. They are often in the wrong position and the penalty in business is lost sales.

Time to write out your playbook. <u>Start with looking at your current situation and setting your priorities and the direction of your company</u>. What is your company known for today? Your marketing needs to be real, so understanding who you are is important. For example, there is a bar and grill down the street from our offices that is known for its Irish Nachos. The owner of J Gilligan's, Randy Ford, sets Saint Patrick's Day as a priority. He spends marketing dollars promoting his business in March. He told me that most of his annual profits come from the few days around March 17th.

What do you want to be known for tomorrow? If you are building a new product or getting ready to offer a new service, this will also determine the direction of your playbook.

This is also a great time to evaluate your staff when thinking about your marketing plan. Great coaches will learn the strength of their players and draw out plays to highlight those strengths. Sometimes the analysis will lead to moving players over, releasing some players, or picking up new players.

You need to think about factors outside of your control when writing your playbook. Remember my example of how we had to change our plan based on our clients' needs? As I write this book the world is dealing with supply chain issues. This will affect your business in ways you cannot control. But knowing this information helps you plan out your marketing. If you have a product that has a back-order of several months, you want to cycle that product from your marketing efforts. Focus on the products you can fulfill. If your entire business is affected by the supply chain issue, you can write a marketing plan that will get in front of the story. Again, be proactive and not reactive.

I met a business owner at one of our networking events who is struggling with supply chain issues and cannot fulfill his orders. He asked me if he should stop marketing all together until things get back to normal. I told him that is the worst thing he can do for his business. I advised him to create content for social media that addresses the concerns in a way that shows his company cares about his clients. Supply chain issues will not last forever and you want to make sure you keep your brand on the mind of your prospects.

Obstacles create opportunities. What opportunities do you see in your current situation? Look at the strengths of your company against the obstacles and see what areas of service you can provide. Going back to my friend Randy Ford, the world shut down the week before Saint Patrick's Day in 2020. He could have given up and shut his doors, but instead he looked at his team's strength and resources and created a marketing plan that saved his business. He quickly set up a drive-through and started offering curbside pick-up. He reached out to local places that needed food delivered to keep their team safe and healthy.

What strengths do you have that you can highlight? Also know your weaknesses and avoid drawing attention to those areas. I have been managing and working with salespeople for most of my career. What I have learned is that without a plan they will unintentionally start to sell products that cannot be fulfilled. They get in meetings with prospects and in an effort to make the prospect happy they will start to drift in the messaging. If you have a marketing plan that clearly lays out what products you are highlighting and educate your sales team on what products to push and when, you avoid these trouble areas.

Be clear in how you define success and track results. The more specifically you can lay out your objectives, the easier it will be for your team to follow the plan. If I were to tell my team, "Next year I want us to sell more than we sold this year." That would not be a clearly defined objective. A better objective would be to tell them we have a goal to sell twenty new podcasting service agreements in the first six months of the year. The marketing plan would lay out how we plan to promote the service to support sales. We would then track results and report those numbers weekly to the company. I might create a spreadsheet that shows the marketing dollars spent on social media posts and show how many leads we got from the post, followed by how many leads we converted to sales.

Back up your marketing playbook with action items. It's not enough to promote your products or services, you have to make sure everyone is ready to sell the product. Using my podcasting example, if we decided to push podcasting in April, we would train and review the sales pitch with our sales team prior to the campaign. My marketing plan would include scheduled meetings with the sales team in March to discuss the April promotion.

Our graphics team would create ads weeks in advance that would be displayed on our website, in digital marketing, on our social media (both organically and paid,) and perhaps in pop-up displays that guests see when they visit one of our studios to do an interview.

We would have to plan for fulfillment expecting an increase in sales. Our production team might hire an additional audio engineer to handle the workload. That would include more training with the onboarding of new staff.

Do you see the value in planning ahead? With no plan you are tempted to make a quick decision and roll out a new product in two weeks. Your sales team is frustrated because they don't have the time to fully understand the new product. There is no proper promotion because your graphics team was not prepared for the new plan and your social media team is scrambling trying to push out something they don't fully understand. If you do close new business, your new clients are frustrated because fulfillment is taking longer than promised.

I speak from experience. I have been guilty of doing that in my career. I have learned the hard way that great ideas are dead on arrival without the proper planning.

Allocate a budget for your plan. How much should you spend on marketing? The US Small Business Administration recommends that small businesses, that is businesses with less than five million in gross revenue, allocate between seven to eight percent of total revenue to marketing. That is assuming your business has margins in the range of 10 to 12 percent.

If you are not making a profit, or your margins are tighter, you still need to spend some money on marketing. Start small with budgets you can control, like social media boosts or pay-per-click ads. But if you spend zero dollars you can expect to get little to no results. Henry Ford is famously quoted as saying, "A man who stops advertising to save money is like a man who stops a clock to save time."

Beyond budgeting for the campaign, make sure you budget for fulfillment and training.

Forecast results. A marketing plan is a part of your overall budget. When you are planning your marketing, what results are you expecting? In the same way you budget for the added expense, you need to include the results of the efforts.

Measure the plan on a regular basis against your benchmarks. Remember to have a baseline before beginning any marketing strategy. But track the campaign on a weekly basis to see if it is yielding the desired result. All marketing efforts take time, so be patient, but be smart. We have discussed that buying a radio or television ad takes at least thirteen weeks before the results start to come in on a regular basis. You are looking for a two-to-one return on your investment. If you spend one dollar on advertising, you should receive two dollars back in sales. Some businesses demand a higher ROI, but I think a two-to-one ROI is a reasonable goal. According to Nielsen, the national average return for every $1.00 spent on media is $1.06. But the most effective advertisers see a $2.09 return for every $1.00 spent. Reread the chapter on advertising to learn how to write an effective ad.

Paul R. Smith created an excellent guide to helping you develop a marketing plan. SOSTAC is an acronym for Situation, Objectives, Strategy, Tactics, Actions, and Control. Go to sostac.org to learn more about the plan, but it asks five basic questions.

1. Where are we now?
2. Where do we want to be?
3. How do we get there?
4. What do we need to get there?
5. How do we monitor performance?

The Marketing Calendar

A MARKETING CALENDAR helps your company stay organized and plan accordingly. Look at the full year from January to December and start strategizing what you want to promote throughout the year.

Going back to your marketing plan, what is your sales cycle? Certain times of the year you will want to push out your big items. Other times you will promote seasonal products.

Think about your target demographic. What is on their mind when you are marketing to them? Try to craft your messaging to get their attention.

What dates are on the calendar that you want to promote? Do you have a Valentine's special you can offer? Maybe something related to the summer travel season? Maybe you want to offer a promotion on the anniversary of your company?

How long do you want to run your campaigns? And what pre-planning is needed to launch the campaigns? This is all in your marketing plan, a calendar just helps you lay it all out and make sure your team is hitting important deadlines.

Conclusion

MEDIA IS RAPIDLY changing, but it does matter. It is still the best way to get the word out about your business and increase your sales.

You need to market your company, but you don't have to waste your money. There is a better way. It starts with understanding who is doing business with you today and then marketing to other prospects who fit a similar profile. Demographics are far more important than the total number of impressions. Have a marketing plan in place before you decide where to spend your marketing dollars. Use the knowledge you have gained from this book to ask the right questions.

Make sure your website is searchable, and that you can be easily located online.

Consider a content marketing strategy. It is the most affordable form of marketing and above all other forms of marketing it builds the most loyal followers to your brand. Remember content marketing is 80 percent providing something of value and 20 percent promotion.

If you are looking for specific marketing advice for your company, I encourage you to visit our website at cenpostmedia.com and click on the contact us button. Our passion is helping businesses with their media needs, and we would love to help you.

ACKNOWLEDGMENTS

My LIFE VERSE is found in Colossians 3:23, HCSB, "Whatever you do, do it enthusiastically, as something done for the Lord and not for men." I also like James 1:7a, HCSB, "Every generous act and every perfect gift is from above." All glory and honor belongs to the Lord. I am nothing without God's grace and mercy through the saving power of the blood of Jesus Christ. John 3:16.

I am blessed with a tremendous support system. At the top of that list is my biggest cheerleader Stacia, my bride of more than twenty years. She has encouraged me in this project like she has encouraged me in my career. Thank you for the countless hours you listened to me read chapters of this book to you as I completed them and your words of affirmation along the way.

Being a dad is my favorite title in the world. I am so proud of both my girls. Katelyn, who graduated high school a year early and got accepted to Texas Tech, is my business girl, always asking me questions about the company. I know she is going to be a great business leader one day, no matter where her career takes her. Trinity is my creative daughter, who knows how to make me laugh. She has such an incredible stage presence, whether it's playing the bass in orchestra or performing in her school play. I love you girls more than words can express. Thanks for putting up with this project and my "do not disturb dad while he is writing" rules.

I want to thank my publisher, Tom Freiling, who believed in me and reached out and asked me to write this book and my copyeditor Christen M. Jeschke.

A huge thank you to Julia Grubb, my assistant. Julia, you are a rock star. There would be no book without the hours you spent researching the topics and editing the first manuscript. You also encouraged me along the way and helped me brainstorm. I am so blessed to have an assistant with a degree in journalism.

A special thanks goes to Ed Frazier. Ed is my mentor, business partner, investor, and friend. Ed, I am so glad you asked me to move my family back to Arlington to work for you in 2009. Grateful that you asked me to come over and run your companies in 2013. Your trust in me is humbling. I want to prove you right every day I come to the office. I can't thank you enough for the countless hours you have spent listening to my problems, encouraging me, and teaching the business. I am forever indebted to yours and Gloria's generosity.

There are so many people in our company that encouraged me to do this project. Thank you to my leadership team Ryan Raines, Rosaline Ogbechie, Ryan Rives, Mark MacGregor, and a special thanks to Scott Peterson, who encouraged me to practice what we preach and start doing content marketing myself. Without your nudging this book would not have happened.

The chapters of this book are full of information I have learned over a twenty-year career in media. Knowledge I learned from mentors and colleagues along the way. Bob James was one of my first Program Directors when I started working in radio. I can still hear him saying, "Miller, you have to pay your dues." Well Bob, I think I am still working to pay my dues. Thanks for taking a chance on a nineteen-year-old kid and being patient with me. Barry Rose also worked at the same radio station. He was our midday DJ and taught me that it doesn't matter where you are working, if you put your name on a project, you had better give it your best. Barry, I still think about that every time I go on-air.

John Morris is the "Voice of the Baylor Bears," but if you met John, he would tell you that title belongs to the late Frank Fallon. That speaks to Morris's humility. John, you treated me like an equal when I emailed you as a college senior. I will never forget that, and I pray I pay it forward to other young men and women trying to break into the business.

Ron Harris was the General Manager of KCBI and modelled for me the importance of integrity. Thank you for pouring into me and my family. And for taking me to India, an experience I will always treasure.

There are so many names of people who I have worked with that have each taught me things about work and life. Dallas Huston, Bill Fishback, Don and Bonnie Dillard, Jimmy Aiken, Gary Moss, Don Day, Dennis Page, Johanna Fisher, Ray Raley, Dale Weller, John McKinnon, Tim Larson, Steve Lehman, Tom Ashley, Robert "Sully" Sullivan, Bill Byrd, Chip Harwood, Dave Curlee, Frank Raphel, Gary Leland, George King, John Goldhammer, Randy Singer, and so many more.

Finally, I want to thank the family and friends who have known about this project and given me words of encouragement along the way. Writing a book is no easy task and your support meant a lot to me. CA and Kathy Miller, Linda Allison, David and Mandy Allison, Jason and Adrienne Ingram, Chris Byrum, and Clayton Aker.

REFERENCES & RESOURCES

CHAPTER ONE

Barnes, B. (2021, August 12). *Disney+ reaches 116 million subscribers, and its parks division returns to profitability.* The New York Times. Retrieved August 27, 2021, from https://www.nytimes.com/2021/08/12/business/disney-plus-subscribers.html.

Flint, J. (2014, May 1). *AT&T interested in acquiring satellite broadcaster DIRECTV.* Los Angeles Times. Retrieved August 27, 2021, from https://www.latimes.com/entertainment/envelope/cotown/la-et-ct-directv-att-20140430-story.html.

Mailchimp. (2021). *Email Marketing Benchmarks and Statistics by Industry.* Mailchimp. Retrieved September 17, 2021, from https://mailchimp.com/resources/email-marketing benchmarks/.

Milliot, J. (2021, January 7). *Print Book Sales Rose 8.2% in 2020.* PublishersWeekly.com. Retrieved August 27, 2021, from https://www.publishersweekly.com/pw/by-topic/industry-news/bookselling/article/85256-print-unit-sales-rose-8-2-in-2020.html.

NDMU. (2018, March 22). *History of Blogging.* NDMU Online. Retrieved September 17, 2021, from https://online.ndm.edu/news/communication/history-of-blogging/.

Watson, A. (2021, September 7). *Print book unit sales in the U.S. 2004-2020*. Statista. Retrieved September 17, 2021, from https://www.statista.com/statistics/422595/print-book-sales-usa/.

CHAPTER TWO

Barthel, M., & Worden, K. (2021, July 16). *Newspaper Fact Sheet*. Pew Research Center's Journalism Project. Retrieved September 24, 2021, from https://www.pewresearch.org/journalism/fact-sheet/newspapers/.

Popik, B. (2019, October 19). *I Never Argue with a Man Who Buys Ink by the Barrel*. Quote Investigator. Retrieved September 24, 2021, from https://quoteinvestigator.com/2018/04/24/ink/.

CHAPTER THREE

Adgate, B. (2020, September 10). *Nielsen To Start Measuring Audio Listening On Headphones*. Forbes. Retrieved September 10, 2021, from https://www.forbes.com/sites/bradadgate/2020/09/10/nielsen-to-start-measuring-audio-listening-on-headphones/.

Deshpande, I. (2020, December 10). *What Is Programmatic Advertising? Definition, Types, Channel, and Advantages*. Toolbox. Retrieved September 10, 2021, fromhttps://www.toolbox.com/marketing/programmatic-advertising/articles/what-is-programmatic-advertising/.

Editors of Encyclopaedia Britannica. (n.d.). *Golden Age of American Radio*. Encyclopaedia Britannica. Retrieved September 10, 2021, from https://www.britannica.com/topic/Golden-Age-of-American-radio.

Insider Intelligence. (2021, July 29). *Podcast Industry Report: Market Growth and Advertising Statistics in 2021*. Insider Intelligence. Retrieved September 10, 2021, from https://www.insiderintelligence.com/insights/the-podcast-industry-report-statistics/.

Locke, T. (2021, April 4). *Mark Cuban on the company that made him a billionaire: Why I knew it would succeed despite many naysayers*. CNBC. Retrieved September 10, 2021, from https://www.cnbc.com/2021/04/04/ billionaire-mark-cuban-on-success-with-broadcast-dot-com.html.

Looking to make an impact? SiriusXM. (n.d.). Retrieved September 10, 2021, from https://www.siriusxm.com/advertise.

The Nielsen Company. (2013). Terminology and Definitions for the Nielsen Radio Diary Service.

Public Broadcasting Service. (n.d.). *The Developmentof Radio.* American Experience. Retrieved September 10, 2021, from https://www.pbs.org/wgbh/americanexperience/ features/rescue-development-radio/.

Smithsonian. (2021, June 16). *The Historical Legacy of Juneteenth.* National Museum of African American History and Culture. Retrieved September 10, 2021, from https:// nmaahc.si.edu/blog-post/historical-legacy-juneteenth.

Statista Research Department. (2021, July 2). *U.S. Radio Industry - Statistics & Facts.* Statista. Retrieved September 10, 2021, from https://www.statista.com/topics/1330/radio/.

Statista Research Department. (2021, June 10). *Most popular music streaming services in the U.S. 2018-2019, by audience.* Statista. Retrieved September 10, 2021, from https:// www.statista.com/statistics/798125/most-popular-us- music-streaming-services-ranked-by-audience/.

CHAPTER FOUR

4K resolution. (n.d.). In *Wikipedia.* Retrieved September 17, 2021, from https://en.wikipedia.org/wiki/4K_resolution.

ATSC 3.0. (n.d.). In *Wikipedia.* Retrieved September 17, 2021, from https://en.wikipedia.org/wiki/ATSC_3.0.

Digital subchannel. (n.d.). In *Wikipedia.* Retrieved September 17, 2021, from https://en.wikipedia.org/wiki/Digital_subchannel.

Fitzgerald, T. (2021, May 27). *The Number Of Cord Cutters And Cord Nevers Has Tripled Since 2014.* Forbes. Retrieved September 17, 2021, from https://www.forbes.com/sites/tonifitzgerald/2021/05/27/the- number-of-cord-cutters-and-cord-nevers-has-tripled-since-2014/.

Hallmark Channel. (n.d.). In *Wikipedia*. Retrieved September 17, 2021, from https://en.wikipedia.org/wiki/Hallmark_Channel.

History of Cable. California Cable & Telecommunications Association. (n.d.). Retrieved September 17, 2021, from https://calcable.org/learn/history-of-cable/.

Iconoscope. (n.d.). In *Wikipedia*. Retrieved September 17, 2021, from https://en.wikipedia.org/wiki/Iconoscope.

Local TV Measurement. Nielsen. (n.d.). Retrieved September 17, 2021, from https://www.nielsen.com/us/en/ solutions/capabilities/local-tv-measurement/.

Perry, A. (2009). *Must-Carry Rules*. The First Amendment Encyclopedia. Retrieved September 17, 2021, from https://www.mtsu.edu/ first-amendment/article/1000/must-carry-rules.

Porter, R. (2019, October 5). *TV Long View: A Guide to the Ever-Expanding World of Ratings Data*. The Hollywood Reporter. Retrieved September 17, 2021, from https://www.hollywoodreporter.com/tv/tv-news/ tv-ratings-explained-a-guide-what-data-all-means-1245591/.

Satellite television. (n.d.). In *Wikipedia*. Retrieved September 17, 2021, from https://en.wikipedia.org/wiki/Satellite_television.

Stewart, D. (2020, June 22). *Antenna TV Has Surprising Staying Power*. The Wall Street Journal. Retrieved September 17, 2021, from https://deloitte.wsj.com/articles/antenna-tv-has-surprising-staying-power-01592852526.

Television antenna. (n.d.). In *Wikipedia*. Retrieved September 17, 2021, from https://en.wikipedia.org/wiki/Television_antenna.

Video camera tube. (n.d.). In *Wikipedia*. Retrieved September 17, 2021, from https://en.wikipedia.org/wiki/Video_camera_tube.

Vlku, N. (2002, May 7). *The History of Television (or, How Did This Get So Big?)*. Television and the Passive Consumer. Retrieved September 17, 2021, from http://www.cs.cornell.edu/~pjs54/ Teaching/AutomaticLifestyle-S02/Projects/Vlku/history.html.

CHAPTER FIVE

Campaign. (2016, January 28). *History of advertising: No 160: The first radio commercials.* Campaign US. Retrieved September 24, 2021, from https://www.campaignlive.com/article/history-advertising-no-160-first-radio-commercials/1381044.

Castonguay, S. (2006, November). *50 Years of the Video Cassette Recorder.* World Intellectual Property Organization. Retrieved December 1, 2021, from https://www.wipo.int/wipo_magazine/en/2006/06/article_0003.html.

Digital Video Recorders (DVR)—An Interesting History. CCTV Camera World. (n.d.). Retrieved September 24, 2021, from https://www.cctvcameraworld.com/digital-video-recorders-history.html.

Energizer. (n.d.). *Hop Back Through Time with The Energizer® Bunny™* Energizer Bunny Timeline. Retrieved September 24, 2021, from https://www.energizer.com/energizer-bunny/bunny-timeline.

Guttmann, A. (2021, April 14). *TV advertising in the U.S.— statistics & facts.* Statista. Retrieved September 24, 2021, from https://www.statista.com/topics/5052/television-advertising-in-the-us/.

Kovalenko, I. (2020, August 4). *What Is Brand Advertising and How to Start Branding Campaign?* SmartyAds. Retrieved September 24, 2021, from https://smartyads.com/blog/what-is-brand-advertising/.

Mertes, A. (2021, May 6). *The History of TV Commercials: From Super Bowl Ads to Funny Ads We Still Love Watching.* Quality Logo Products. Retrieved September 24, 2021, from https://www.qualitylogoproducts.com/promo-university/history-of-tv-ads.htm.

Mertes, A. (2021, September 8). *The 10 Greatest TV Commercials of All Time.* Quality Logo Products Blog. Retrieved September 24, 2021, from https://www.qualitylogoproducts.com/blog/10-memorable-tv-commercials/.

Report: Radio Ad Spend Expected to Drop 17% This Year, Before Rebounding In 2021. InsideRadio. (2020, October 7). Retrieved September 24, 2021, from http://www.insideradio.com/free/report-radio-ad-spend-expected-to-drop-17-this-year-before-rebounding-in-2021/article_f5eb66ac-0861-11eb-9796-07ffd7fe7a39.html.

Stoll, J. (2021, June 24). *Weekly time spent watching live TV in the U.S. 2021*. Statista. Retrieved September 24, 2021, from https://www.statista.com/statistics/707084/time-spent-live-tv/.

What was the 'Share a Coke' campaign? Coca-Cola Australia. (n.d.). Retrieved September 24, 2021, from https://www.coca-colacompany.com/au/faqs/what-was-the-share-a-coke-campaign.

CHAPTER SIX

Apple TV. (n.d.). In *Wikipedia*. Retrieved October 1, 2021, from https://en.wikipedia.org/wiki/Apple_TV.

Apple. (2007, March 21). Apple TV Now Shipping. *Apple Newsroom*. Retrieved October 1, 2021, from https://www.apple.com/newsroom/2007/03/21Apple-TV-Now-Shipping/.

Chevalier, S. (2021, July 7). *Number of Amazon Prime subscribers in the U.S. 2014-2021*. Statista. Retrieved October 1, 2021, from https://www.statista.com/statistics/1223385/amazon-prime-subscribers-in-the-united-states/.

Cook, S. (2021, May 13). *Cord Cutting Statistics and Trends in 2021*. Comparitech. Retrieved October 1, 2021, from https://www.comparitech.com/tv-streaming/cord-cutting-statistics/.

Coppola, D. (2021, November 23). *Amazon total paying Prime members 2020*. Statista. Retrieved December 1, 2021, from https://www.statista.com/statistics/829113/number-of-paying-amazon-prime-members/.

Enfroy, A. (2021, November 29). *7+ Best OTT Platforms of 2022 (Ranked and Reviewed)*. Adam Enfroy. Retrieved December 2, 2021, from https://www.adamenfroy.com/ott-platform.

Gambino, R. (2021, February 11). *Guide to launching a fast channel*. Harmonic. Retrieved October 1, 2021, from https://www.harmonicinc.com/insights/blog/fast-channel.

Going Swimmingly: Streaming Continues to Grow Among Consumers. Nielsen. (2020, August 24). Retrieved October 1, 2021, from https://www.nielsen.com/us/en/insights/article/2020/streaming-video-aug-2020-milestone/.

Google. (2010, May 20). Industry Leaders Announce Open Platform to Bring Web to TV. *News from Google*. Retrieved October 1, 2021, from http://googlepress.blogspot.com/2010/05/industry-leaders-announce-open-platform.html.

Han, J. (2020, September 22). *The History of OTT...So Far*. Matterkind. Retrieved October 1, 2021, from https://matterkind.com/insights/the-history-of-ott-so-far/.

Hayes, D. (2021, August 5). *ViacomCBS Global Streaming Subscribers Top 42M, Up 6.5M In Q2, Powered By Paramount+* Deadline. Retrieved October 1, 2021, from https://deadline.com/2021/08/viacomcbs-global-streaming-subscribers-42-million-paramount-plus-1234809133/.

Horn, L. (2014, April 2). *Fire TV: Everything You Need to Know About Amazon's $100 Streaming Box*. Gizmodo. Retrieved October 1, 2021, from https://gizmodo.com/amazons-fire-tv-everything-you-need-to-know-1556889628.

Hughes, D. (2021, October 12). *The Beginner's Guide to Programmatic Advertising*. Digital Marketing Institute. Retrieved December 2, 2021, from https://digitalmarketinginstitute.com/blog/the-beginners-guide-to-programmatic-advertising.

Munson, B. (2021, April 22). *AT&T loses 620,000 video subs in Q1 as DirecTV deal moves ahead*. Fierce Video. Retrieved October 1, 2021, from https://www.fiercevideo.com/video/at-t-loses-620-000-video-subs-q1-as-directv-deal-moves-ahead.

Opam, K. (2014, June 25). *Google officially unveils Android TV*. The Verge. Retrieved October 1, 2021, from https://www.theverge.com/2014/6/25/5840424/google-announces-android-tv.

Programmatic Media Buying | Definition. Adjust. (n.d.).
Retrieved October 1, 2021, from https://www.adjust.
com/glossary/programmatic-media-buying/.

Rifilato, T. (2021, July 29). *Peacock Hits 54 Million Subscribers
With Help From The Olympics.* AdExchanger. Retrieved
October 1, 2021, from https://www.adexchanger.
com/ad-exchange-news/peacock-hits-54-million-
subscribers-with-help-from-the-olympics/.

Roku App Store Statistics and Trends 2021. 42matters. (2021, August
27). Retrieved October 1, 2021, from https://42matters.
com/roku-app-store-statistics-and-trends.

Shahzeidi, A. (2021, April 9). *11 Best OTT Platforms for 2021 (Pricing
& Features Included).* Uscreen. Retrieved October 1, 2021,
from https://www.uscreen.tv/blog/ott-platforms/.

Spangler, T. (2021, January 22). *Apple TV Plus' Freeloader Problem: 62%
of Subscribers Are on Free Offers.* Variety. Retrieved October
1, 2021, from https://variety.com/2021/digital/news/apple-
tv-plus-freeloader-problem-percent-free-1234890385/.

Stoll, J. (2021, June 28). *Projected users of Apple TV Plus in the U.S. 2020.*
Statista. Retrieved October 1, 2021, from https://www.statista.com/
statistics/1136261/number-of-apple-tv-plus-subscribers-us/.

Stoll, J. (2021, March 31). *Global AVoD spend 2019-2025, by country.*
Statista. Retrieved October 1, 2021, from https://www.statista.
com/statistics/1125739/countries-by-avod-revenue/.

Stoll, J. (2021, November 15). *Disney+ subscriber numbers
worldwide 2020-2021.* Statista. Retrieved December 1,
2021, from https://www.statista.com/statistics/1095372/
disney-plus-number-of-subscribers-us/.

Stoll, J. (2021, November 15). *Number of Hulu's paying subscribers
in the U.S. 2019-2021, by quarter.* Statista. Retrieved
December 1, 2021, from https://www.statista.com/
statistics/258014/number-of-hulus-paying-subscribers/.

Stoll, J. (2021, November 24). *Roku monthly active users in the U.S. 2016-2021.* Statista. Retrieved December 2, 2021, from https://www.statista.com/statistics/714052/roku-monthly-streamers.

Stoll, J. (2021, October 22). *Netflix subscribers count worldwide 2011-2020.* Statista. Retrieved October 29, 2021, from https://www.statista.com/statistics/250934/quarterly-number-of-netflix-streaming-subscribers-worldwide/.

Stoll, J. (2021, October 27). *Number of HBO and HBO Max subscribers in the U.S. 2019-2021.* Statista. Retrieved December 1, 2021, from https://www.statista.com/statistics/539290/hbo-now-subscribers/.

Tariq, H. (2021, February 8). *What Is OTT Advertising, And Why Is It A Trend?* Forbes. Retrieved October 1, 2021, from https://www.forbes.com/sites/forbescommunicationscouncil/2021/02/08/what-is-ott-advertising-and-why-is-it-a-trend/.

The ultimate guide to programmatic advertising. Bannerflow. (n.d.). Retrieved October 1, 2021, from https://www.bannerflow.com/inspiration/ultimate-guides/programmatic-advertising/#how-do-you-buy-programmatically.

What is OTT? Endavo Media. (n.d.). Retrieved October 1, 2021, from https://www.endavomedia.com/what-is-ott/.

CHAPTER SEVEN

Andrews, E. (2019, October 28). *Who Invented the Internet?* History.com. Retrieved October 8, 2021, from https://www.history.com/news/who-invented-the-internet.

Armstrong, M. (2021, August 6). *How Many Websites Are There?* Statista. Retrieved October 8, 2021, from https://www.statista.com/chart/19058/number-of-websites-online/.

The Beginner's Guide to Google Analytics. Moz Pro. (n.d.). Retrieved October 8, 2021, from https://moz.com/beginners-guide-to-google-analytics.

Chapa, K. (2021, November 9). *Top 10 Important SEO Techniques of 2022*. Delta Marketing Group. Retrieved December 2, 2021, from https://www.godelta.com/blog/important-seo-techniques.

Digital Marketing Institute. (2021, October 18). *What Is SEO & Why Is It Important?* Digital Marketing Institute. Retrieved December 2, 2021, from https://digitalmarketinginstitute. com/blog/what-is-seo-and-why-is-it-important.

Forbes Agency Council. (2021, May 4). *11 SEO Trends And Changes That Will Impact Business In 2021*. Forbes. Retrieved October 8, 2021, from https://www.forbes.com/ sites/forbesagency council/2021/05/04/11-seo-trends- and-changes-that-will-impact-business-in-2021/.

Galov, N. (2021, July 4). *What Percentage of Small Businesses Have a Website*. Review42. Retrieved October 8, 2021, from https://review42.com/ resources/what-percentage-of-small-businesses-have-a-website/.

Google. (2021, November 22). *Search Engine Optimization (SEO) Starter Guide*. Google Search Central. Retrieved December 2, 2021, from https://developers.google. com/search/docs/beginner/seo-starter-guide.

The History of Search Engines. WordStream. (n.d.). Retrieved October 8, 2021, from https://www.wordstream.com/ articles/internet-search-engines-history.

Jones, D. (2021, July 28). *8 Expert Tips to Build a Winning SEO Strategy in 2021*. WordStream. Retrieved October 8, 2021, from https:// www.wordstream.com/blog/ws/2021/03/05/seo-strategy.

Lynch, O. (2020, July 12). *The 12 Best PPC Ad Networks 2020*. CHEQ. Retrieved October 8, 2021, from https:// www.cheq.ai/12-best-ppc-ad-networks.

McCormick, K. (2020, November 17). *15 Ways to Make Your Website More Visible on Google (and Elsewhere)*. WordStream. Retrieved October 8, 2021, from https://www.wordstream.com/blog/ws/2020/11/17/ website-visibility.

Samanta, J. (2019, March 30). *How Google Analytics Help Small Business Owners to Make Better Business Decisions.* Entrepreneur. Retrieved October 8, 2021, from https://www.entrepreneur.com/article/331526.

Search engine marketing. Optimizely. (n.d.). Retrieved October 8, 2021, from https://www.optimizely.com/optimization-glossary/search-engine-marketing/.

Shewan, D. (2021, November 17). *How Much Does Google Ads Cost?* WordStream. Retrieved December 2, 2021, from https://www.wordstream.com/blog/ws/2015/05/21/how-much-does-adwords-cost.

A Short History of the Internet. National Science and Media Museum. (2020, December 3). Retrieved October 8, 2021, from https://www.scienceandmediamuseum.org.uk/objects-and-stories/short-history-internet.

The Wix Team. (2017, January 16). *What is Backlinking and Why Is it Important for SEO?* Wix Blog. Retrieved October 8, 2021, from https://www.wix.com/blog/2017/01/what-is-backlinking-and-why-is-it-important-for-seo/.

Total number of Websites. Internet Live Stats. (n.d.). Retrieved October 8, 2021, from https://www.internetlivestats.com/total-number-of-websites/.

CHAPTER EIGHT

Baer, J. (n.d.). *Is Twitter for Business Even Worth the Trouble?* Convince & Convert. Retrieved October 15, 2021, from https://www.convinceandconvert.com/social-media-strategy/is-twitter-for-business-even-worth-the-trouble/.

Bendall, C. (n.d.). *16 Statistics to Show Why Instagram Marketing is Crucial.* Our Social Times. Retrieved October 15, 2021, from https://oursocialtimes.com/16-statistics-to-show-why-marketers-need-instagram/.

Bump, P. (2021, March 22). *31 LinkedIn Stats That Marketers Need to Know in 2021.* HubSpot Blog. Retrieved October 15, 2021, from https://blog.hubspot.com/marketing/linkedin-stats.

Case Studies. Instagram for Business. (n.d.). Retrieved October 15, 2021, from https://business.instagram.com/success.

Chawlani, Y. (2021, April 6). *How to Use Instagram for Business in 2021*. Business 2 Community. Retrieved October 15, 2021, from https://www.business2community.com/instagram/how-to-use-instagram-for-business-in-2021-02396387.

Chen, J. (2020, July 30). *Expert tips on using Facebook for your small business*. Sprout Social. Retrieved October 15, 2021, from https://sproutsocial.com/insights/facebook-for-small-business/.

The Evolution of Social Media: How Did It Begin, and Where Could It Go Next? Maryville University. (n.d.). Retrieved October 15, 2021, from https://online.maryville.edu/blog/evolution-social-media/.

Hart, K. (2021, June 14). *The next big social network: Nextdoor*. Axios. Retrieved October 15, 2021, from https://www.axios.com/the-next-big-social-network-nextdoor-2bc336aa-e50b-4ea8-b097-f273bd5994d6.html.

How to create a Twitter marketing strategy for your brand. Sprout Social. (n.d.). Retrieved October 15, 2021, from https://sproutsocial.com/twitter-marketing/.

Iqbal, M. (2021, November 12). *LinkedIn Usage and Revenue Statistics (2021)*. Business of Apps. Retrieved December 2, 2021, from https://www.businessofapps.com/data/linkedin-statistics/.

Lessard, K. (2019, December 22). *How to Boost Your B2B Content Strategy and the New, Free LinkedIn Page Feature that Can Help*. LinkedIn Marketing Blog. Retrieved October 15, 2021, from https://www.linkedin.com/business/marketing/blog/content-marketing/the-ultimate-guide-to-improve-your-b2b-content-marketing-strategy.

LinkedIn Marketing Solutions. (n.d.). The Case for B2B Marketing on LinkedIn.

McCoy, T. (2020, June 17). *Announcing Business Posts: Get the Word Out Locally About Your Business*. Nextdoor Business. Retrieved October 15,

2021, from https://business.nextdoor.com/local/resources/announcing-business-posts-get-the-word-out-locally-about-your-business.

Mohsin, M. (2021, March 14). *10 Snapchat Statistics You Need to Know in 2021 [Infographic]*. Oberlo. Retrieved October 15, 2021, from https://www.oberlo.com/blog/snapchat-statistics.

Newberry, C. (2021, January 11). *47 Facebook Stats That Matter to Marketers in 2021*. Hootsuite Blog. Retrieved October 15, 2021, from https://blog.hootsuite.com/facebook-statistics/.

Newberry, C., & McLachlan, S. (2020, March 8). *Facebook Marketing in 2021: How to Use Facebook for Business*. Hootsuite Blog. Retrieved October 15, 2021, from https://blog.hootsuite.com/facebook-marketing-tips/.

Nextdoor Editorial Team. (2020, July 1). *Dashboard: Measure Your Success on Nextdoor*. Nextdoor Business. Retrieved October 15, 2021, from https://business.nextdoor.com/local/resources/dashboard-measure-your-success-on-nextdoor.

Olafson, K. (2020, March 11). *Snapchat for Business: The Ultimate Marketing Guide*. Hootsuite Blog. Retrieved October 15, 2021, from https://blog.hootsuite.com/snapchat-for-business-guide/.

Olafson, K. (2020, October 8). *21 Snapchat Stats That Matter to Social Media Marketers*. Hootsuite Blog. Retrieved October 15, 2021, from https://blog.hootsuite.com/snapchat-statistics-for-business/.

Rynne, A. (2021, August 19). *Now Is the Time to Make LinkedIn a Strategic Priority. Here's Why*. LinkedIn Marketing Blog. Retrieved October 15, 2021, from https://www.linkedin.com/business/marketing/blog/linkedin-ads/why-you-should-be-marketing-on-linkedin-right-now.

Shah, S. (2016, May 14). *The history of social networking*. Digital Trends. Retrieved October 15, 2021, from https://www.digitaltrends.com/features/the-history-of-social-networking/. Southern, M. (2021, January 15). *TikTok Beats Facebook in Time Spent Per User*. Search Engine Journal. Retrieved October 15, 2021, from https://www.searchenginejournal.com/tiktok-beats-facebook-in-time-spent-per-user/392643/.

Statista Research Department. (2021, July 23). *Twitter: annual ad spend 2014-2020*. Statista. Retrieved October 15, 2021, from https://www.statista.com/statistics/685637/twitter-ad-cost/.

Statista Research Department. (2021, October 19). *Leading U.S. Twitter advertisers in Q1 2020, by ad spend*. Statista. Retrieved December 2, 2021, from https://www.statista.com/statistics/1112281/us-twitter-advertisers-ranked-by-ad-spend/.

Tobin, J. (2021, February 19). *Five Upcoming Social Networks To Keep An Eye On In 2021*. Forbes. Retrieved October 15, 2021, from https://www.forbes.com/sites/forbesagencycouncil/2021/02/19/five-upcoming-social-networks-to-keep-an-eye-on-in-2021.

Williams, W. (2020, July 23). *Is Twitter Worth It for Brands? We Say No.* First Page Strategy. Retrieved October 15, 2021, from https://www.firstpagestrategy.com/blog/is-twitter-worth-it-for-brands.

CHAPTER NINE

Aghajanian, S. (2021, September 17). *Mobile Push Notifications: An Absolute Necessity for Mobile App Marketing*. VWO Blog. Retrieved October 22, 2021, from https://vwo.com/blog/mobile-push-notifications/.

Andrus, A. (2018, January 25). *How Does Remarketing on Google AdWords Work?* Disruptive Advertising. Retrieved October 22, 2021, from https://disruptiveadvertising.com/ppc/remarketing/.

Chen, J. (2020, September 17). *What is influencer marketing: How to develop your strategy*. Sprout Social. Retrieved October 22, 2021, from https://sproutsocial.com/insights/influencer-marketing/.

Clark, D. (2012, November 11). *The End of the Expert: Why No One in Marketing Knows What they're Doing*. Forbes. Retrieved October 22, 2021, from http://www.forbes.com/sites/dorieclark/2012/11/11/the-end-of-the-expert-why-no-one-in-marketing-knows-what-theyre-doing/.

Cox, L. (2021, August 25). *26 Examples of Brilliant Email Marketing Campaigns [Template]*. HubSpot Blog. Retrieved October 22, 2021, from https://blog.hubspot.com/marketing/email-marketing-examples-list.

DJ Team. (2020, December 18). *What are Examples of Content Marketing on Social Media?* DemandJump. Retrieved October 22, 2021, from https://www.demandjump.com/blog/what-are-examples-of-content-marketing-on-social-media.

Duncan, T. (2020, June 22). *The Power of Email and Mobile Marketing Automation.* Braze. Retrieved October 22, 2021, from https://www.braze.com/resources/articles/email-and-mobile-marketing-automation.

The Evolution of Digital Marketing - What Happened in 3 Decades? W3 Lab. (2020, May 14). Retrieved October 22, 2021, from https://w3-lab.com/evolution-of-digital-marketing/.

Geyser, W. (2021, August 20). *15 Influencer Marketing Examples to Power Your Influencer Campaign Planning.* Influencer Marketing Hub. Retrieved October 22, 2021, from https://influencermarketinghub.com/influencer-marketing-examples/.

Google. (n.d.). *Advertiser guide: Working with third parties.* Google Advertising Policies Help. Retrieved October 22, 2021, from https://support.google.com/adspolicy/answer/9457109?hl=en.

Hamilton, L. (n.d.). *Do You Need to Worry About CAN-SPAM Lawsuits?* Adobe Marketo Engage. Retrieved October 22, 2021, from https://blog.marketo.com/2016/07/do-you-need-to-worry-about-can-spam-lawsuits.html.

Hopkins, J., & Turner, J. (n.d.). *Calculating the ROI of a mobile marketing campaign.* Marketing Dive. Retrieved October 22, 2021, from https://www.marketingdive.com/ex/mobilemarketer/cms/opinion/columns/12526.html.

Hott, A. (2021, March 25). *SMS Marketing: the Good, the Bad, and the Don't You Dare.* OptinMonster. Retrieved October 22, 2021, from https://optinmonster.com/sms-marketing/.

How does Geo targeting Work? GeoEdge. (n.d.). Retrieved October 22, 2021, from https://www.geoedge.com/university/how-does-geo-targeting-work/.

Keskin, S. (2021, September 24). *9 of the Best Email Marketing Examples We've Seen (2021)*. Sleeknote. Retrieved December 2, 2021, from https://sleeknote. com/blog/best-email-marketing-examples.

Knezovic, A. (2021, September 2). *Mobile Marketing and Social Media: How to Leverage Social Media for Your Mobile Campaign?* Udonis. Retrieved October 22, 2021, from https://www.blog.udonis.co/ mobile-marketing/mobile-marketing-and-social-media.

Landis, T. (2021, September 27). *How Content and Email Marketing Work Together to Build Your Business*. OutboundEngine. Retrieved October 22, 2021, from https://www.outboundengine. com/blog/content-marketing-and-email-marketing/.

Lin, Y. (2021, February 4). *Top 10 Digital Marketing Statistics and Facts for 2021 [Infographic]*. Oberlo. Retrieved October 22, 2021, from https://www.oberlo.com/blog/digital-marketing-statistics.

Marketo. (n.d.). *Mobile Marketing New*. Adobe Experience Cloud. Retrieved October 22, 2021, from https:// www.marketo.com/mobile-marketing/.

Moore, K. (n.d.). *Google Advertising Stats for 2021*. Digital Third Coast. Retrieved October 22, 2021, from https://www. digitalthirdcoast.com/blog/google-ads-statistics.

Perricone, C. (2021, July 1). *The Ultimate Guide to PPC Marketing*. HubSpot Blog. Retrieved October 22, 2021, from https://blog.hubspot.com/marketing/ppc.

Schachter, H. (n.d.). *20 Killer Examples of Influencer Marketing*. Travel Mindset. Retrieved October 22, 2021, from https://www.travelmindset.com/20-influencer- marketing-examples/.

Schooley, S. (2021, August 25). *Text Message Marketing: The Ultimate Mobile Engagement Tool*. business.com. Retrieved October 22, 2021, from https://www.business. com/articles/text-message-marketing-benefits/.

Search engine marketing. Optimizely. (n.d.). Retrieved
October 22, 2021, from https://www.optimizely.com/
optimization-glossary/search-engine-marketing/.

Then and Now: The Evolution of Digital Marketing. Compose.
ly. (2020, June 19). Retrieved October 22, 2021, from https://
compose.ly/strategy/evolution-of-digital-marketing/.

Wernet, K. (n.d.). *7 statistics that prove email marketing works for younger
demographics.* Emma Email Marketing. Retrieved October 22,
2021, from https://content.myemma.com/blog/7-statistics-that-
prove-email-marketing-works-for-younger-demographics.

What Is A Digital Marketing Platform? Marketing Evolution.
(n.d.). Retrieved October 22, 2021, from https://www.
marketingevolution.com/marketing-essentials/what-is-
a-digital-marketing-platform-marketing-evolution.

CHAPTER TEN

15 Local SEO Statistics for 2021. Safari Digital. (2020, February
10). Retrieved October 29, 2021, from https://www.
safaridigital.com.au/blog/local-seo-statistics/.

Bassig, M. (2020, September 2). *Yelp Fact Sheet: Stats Your Business
Needs to Know.* ReviewTrackers. Retrieved October 29, 2021,
from https://www.reviewtrackers.com/blog/yelp-factsheet/.

Cox, L. (2020, February 18). *16 Stats That Prove the Importance of
Local SEO.* HubSpot Blog. Retrieved October 29, 2021, from
https://blog.hubspot.com/marketing/local-seo-stats.

Google. (n.d.). *About Google Business Profile.* Google
Business Profile Help. Retrieved October 29,
2021, from https://support.google.com/business/
answer/3038063?hl=en&co=GENIE.Platform%3DAndroid.

The Importance of Keeping Online Business Listings Up to Date. Impact
Group Marketing. (2021, March 24). Retrieved October 29, 2021,
from https://www.impactgroupmarketing.com/blog/articleid/589/
the-importance-of-keeping-online-business-listings-up-to-date.

Irigoyen, D. (2021, June 30). *Google My Business Optimization Tips for 2021*. Designzillas. Retrieved October 29, 2021, from https://www.designzillas.com/blog/ google-my-business-optimization-tips-2021.

Lima, J. (2016, September 5). *140 years since Alexander Graham Bell invented the telephone – so what's changed?* Tech Monitor. Retrieved October 29, 2021, from https://techmonitor.ai/ techonology/hardware/140-years-since-alexander-graham-bell-invented-the-telephone-so-whats-changed-4835831.

McDaniel, M. (n.d.). *A Short History of The Yellow Pages*. Frugal Marketing. Retrieved October 29, 2021, from https://www. frugalmarketing.com/dtb/yellow-pages-history.shtml.

McDermott, A. (2020, December 1). *The Ultimate Guide To Google My Business in 2021*. Grade.us. Retrieved October 29, 2021, from https://blog.grade.us/google-my-business/.

Murphy, R. (2020, December 9). *Local Consumer Review Survey 2020*. BrightLocal. Retrieved October 29, 2021, from https://www. brightlocal.com/research/local-consumer-review-survey/.

Newberry, C. (2021, January 11). *47 Facebook Stats That Matter to Marketers in 2021*. Hootsuite Blog. Retrieved October 29, 2021, from https://blog.hootsuite.com/facebook-statistics/.

Ragon, J. P. (2021, April 23). *7 Reasons To Use Online Directories*. Wilderness Agency. Retrieved October 29, 2021, from https://www.wildernessagency. com/7-reasons-to-use-online-directories/.

Schwartz, A. (2019, June 6). *How to update your business information on Yelp*. Yelp Blog. Retrieved October 29, 2021, from https://blog.yelp. com/businesses/updating-your-business-information-on-yelp/.

Science Reference Section. (2019, November 19). *Who is credited with inventing the telephone?* Library of Congress. Retrieved October 29, 2021, from https://www.loc.gov/everyday-mysteries/ item/who-is-credited-with-inventing-the-telephone/.

Sehl, K. (2020, May 25). *How to Use Google My Business to Get More Customers*. Hootsuite Blog. Retrieved October 29, 2021, from https://blog.hootsuite.com/google-my-business/.

Statler, J. (n.d.). *Top 12 Benefits of a Facebook for Business*. Post Planner. Retrieved October 29, 2021, from https://www. postplanner.com top-10-benefits-facebook-business-page/.

Stella, J. (2021, February 1). *The Importance Of Directories For Online Visibility*. UpCity. Retrieved October 29, 2021, from https://upcity.com/experts/the-importance-of-directories-for-online-visibility/.

Storm, M. (2019, October 26). *Local SEO Stats: 17 Stats to Prove You Need a Local SEO Strategy*. WebFX Blog. Retrieved October 29, 2021, from https://www.webfx.com/blog/seo/local-seo-stats/.

Turner, J. (n.d.). *What is the Importance of Online Directories?* The Search Engine Guys. Retrieved October 29, 2021, from https://www.thesearchengineguys.com/what-is-the-importance-of-online-directories/.

The Yelp Business Handbook. ReviewTrackers. (2021, September 29). Retrieved October 29, 2021, from https://www. reviewtrackers.com/guides/yelp-business/.

CHAPTER ELEVEN

Bump, P. (2021, July 30). *Why Marketers Should Implement User-Generated Content: 23 Stats to Know*. HubSpot Blog. Retrieved November 5, 2021, from https://blog.hubspot.com/marketing/user-generated-content-stats.

Daniel, K. (2021, July 12). *The State of Content Marketing in 2021 [Stats & Trends to Watch]*. HubSpot Blog. Retrieved November 5, 2021, from https://blog.hubspot.com/marketing/state-of-content-marketing-infographic.

Forbes Communications Council. (2021, October 19). *12 Clever Ways For Brands To Leverage User-Generated Content*. Forbes. Retrieved November 5, 2021, from https://www.forbes.com/.

sites/forbescommunicationscouncil/2021/10/19/12-clever-
ways-for-brands-to-leverage-user-generated-content/.

Growth and Opportunities in Content Marketing. Association of National
Advertisers. (2020, July 13). Retrieved November 5, 2021, from https://
www.ana.net/miccontent/show/id/rr-2020-content-marketing.

HubSpot. (n.d.). *The Ultimate List of Marketing Statistics
for 2021*. HubSpot. Retrieved November 5, 2021,from
https://www.hubspot.com marketing-statistics.

Mazouri, H. (2021, July 14). *User-generated content: 5 steps to turn customers
into advocates*. Sprout Social. Retrieved November 5, 2021, from
https://sproutsocial.com/insights/user-generated-content-guide/.

Pandya, N. (2021, November 2). *The whys and hows of user-generated
content*. YourStory Media. Retrieved November 5, 2021, from https://
yourstory.com/2021/10/whys-hows-user-generated-content/amp.

Pulizzi, J. (2016, July 1). *The History of Content Marketing [Updated
Infographic]*. Content Marketing Institute. Retrieved November 5,
2021, from https://contentmarketinginstitute.com/2016/07/history-
content-marketing/.

Speiser, M. (2020, September 4). *A (Brief) History of Content Marketing*.
Knotch Pros & Content. Retrieved November 5, 2021, from https://
prosandcontent.knotch.com/posts/history-of-content-marketing.

Staff Writer. (2021, November 24). *40+ Incredible Content
Marketing Statistics for 2021*. SmallBizGenius. Retrieved
December 2, 2021, from https://www.smallbizgenius.net/
by-the-numbers/content-marketing-statistics/#gref.

Technavio. (2021, June 10). *$ 417.85 Bn Growth in Global Content
Marketing Market 2021-2025 | Growing Demand for Digital
Magazines to be a Major Trend | Technavio*. Cision PR Newswire.
Retrieved November 5, 2021, from https://www.prnewswire.
com/news-releases/-417-85-bn-growth-in-global-content-
marketing-market-2021-2025--growing-demand-for-digital-
magazines-to-be-a-major-trend--technavio-301310563.html.

CHAPTER TWELVE

Cooper, P., & Tien, S. (2021, June 1). *How to Create a Social Media Calendar: Tips and Templates.* Hootsuite Blog. Retrieved November 12, 2021, from https://blog.hootsuite.com/how-to-create-a-social-media-content-calendar/.

Forbes Agency Council. (2019, May 31). *Six Tips For Developing An Effective Marketing Plan.* Forbes. Retrieved November 12, 2021, from https://www.forbes.com/sites/forbesagencycouncil/2019/05/31/six-tips-for-developing-an-effective-marketing-plan/.

Forsey, C. (2021, June 10). *How Much Should Your Marketing Team Budget for 2021? [By Industry].* HubSpot Blog. Retrieved November 12, 2021, from https://blog.hubspot.com/marketing/marketing-budget-percentage.

Lindley, S. (2021, May 25). *How to structure an effective marketing plan.* Smart Insights. Retrieved November 12, 2021, from https://www.smartinsights.com/marketing-planning/create-a-marketing-plan/structure-effective-marketing-plan/.

Pyle, S. (2020). *7 reasons you shouldn't cut your marketing budget in a recession.* The Business Journals. Retrieved November 12, 2021, from https://www.bizjournals.com/bizjournals/how-to/marketing/2020/11/7-reasons-you-shouldn-t-cut-your-marketing-budget.html.

Storm, M. (2021, August 30). *How to Plan a Marketing Calendar: Marketing Calendar in 8 Steps.* WebFX Blog. Retrieved November 12, 2021, from https://www.webfx.com/blog/marketing/how-to-plan-a-marketing-calendar-marketing-calendar/.

Trillo, C. (2021, May 18). *Marketing Calendar: The Definitive Guide & Templates [2021].* Evinex Digital Marketing Agency. Retrieved November 12, 2021, from https://www.evinex.com/marketing-calendar/.

Woschnick, V. (2021, August 11). *What Are the Top 10 Most Effective Marketing Strategies?* Weidert Group. Retrieved November 12, 2021, from https://www.weidert.com/blog/top-10-most-effective-marketing-strategies.

Lightning Source UK Ltd.
Milton Keynes UK
UKHW010639150322
400092UK00002B/253